The Psalms in Christian Worship

A PRACTICAL GUIDE

Massey H. Shepherd Jr.

AUGSBURG PUBLISHING HOUSE
MINNEAPOLIS, MINNESOTA

THE PSALMS IN CHRISTIAN WORSHIP

Copyright © 1976 Augsburg Publishing House

Library of Congress Catalog Card No. 76-3873

International Standard Book No. 0-8066-1533-8

Scripture quotations unless otherwise noted are from the Revised Standard Version of the Bible, copyright 1946, 1952, and 1971 by the Division of Christian Education of the National Council of Churches.

MANUFACTURED IN THE UNITED STATES OF AMERICA

Contents

Preface

This book is designed to help pastors and church musicians in planning and executing the use of the Psalms in the liturgical services of the church. The Psalms are the oldest and most enduring praise and prayer of Christians. The revival of interest in them, in new translations and musical settings, is one of the notable signs of renewal in the worship of the church in our times. Creative innovation in such renewal, however, can only be effective if it is rooted in a sound knowledge of tradition. It is like the "householder who brings out of his treasure what is new and what is old" (Matthew 13:52).

The illustrative translations from the Psalter in this study are by the author. References to them, as also to other passages of Scripture, are according to the Revised Standard Version.

I.

The Formation
of the Psalter

1. The Form of Hebrew Poetry

The Hebrew title of the Psalter is *Tehillim*, "Praises," formed from the same root *hll* as the word "Hallelujah." Our word "psalm" derives from the Greek term *psalmos* (Latin, *psalmus*), which translates the Hebrew *mizmor*, used in the title of 57 Psalms, and refers to a song accompanied by a stringed instrument. In one Greek manuscript the Psalter is entitled *Psalterion*, the term for a harp, somewhat larger than the lyre and often consisting of ten strings.[1]

The Psalter contains only a portion of the religious verse of the Old Testament. It has been estimated that one-third of the Old Testament is in poetic form: not only such poems as the Song of Songs and Lamentations, but also Proverbs, most of Job, and a large portion of the prophetic books. Some of the oldest verse in the Old Testament, older or as old as anything in the Psalter, is found scattered in the historical books: the Testament of Jacob,[2] the Songs of Miriam[3] and of Deborah,[4] and David's laments over Saul and Jonathan and over Abner.[5] A psalm of thanksgiving for victory, attrib-

7

uted to David but reflecting a later time in the
Judaean monarchy, is 2 Samuel 22, which is included in the Psalter, in a slightly different version,
as Psalm 18.

Modern archaeological discoveries have brought to
light much of the religious poetry of the ancient
Near Eastern cultures of Palestine, Babylonia, and
Egypt, with which the Hebrews were in constant
interaction. These provide not only background, but
in many cases parallels to the mythic and cultic
patterns of Hebrew psalmody. In particular, they
show how the Psalms share the same poetic types
and forms in use among their neighbors.[6] We shall
discuss the poetic types in the following section. The
poetic forms or structures are generally known as
"parallelism of verse members." That is, each verse
line is divided into two—sometimes three—parts,
called "stichs," each of which repeats or comple-
ments the thought of the verse.

There are three basic forms of parallelism which
occur most frequently: synonymous, antithetical, and
synthetic. In synonymous parallelism the two parts
or stichs repeat the same thought, although in some
cases the second part introduces an additional dimen-
sion of meaning:

> The LORD is my light and my salvation:
>> whom shall I fear?
> The LORD is the strength of my life:
>> of whom shall I be afraid? (27:1)

> The heavens declare the glory of God;
>> the vault of the sky shows his handiwork.
>>> (19:1)

In the second example, the word "handiwork" adds the note that the heavens not only show God's glory but are his creation.

The antithetical form provides a contrasting thought between the first and second stichs:

> For the LORD knows the way of the just;
>> but the way of the wicked will perish.
>>> (1:6)

> Though my father and mother have forsaken me,
>> the LORD will uphold me. (27:10)

An interesting example from the New Testament is contained in the Song of Mary, the *Magnificat*, in Luke 2:52-53:

> He has put down the mighty from their thrones,
>> and exalted those of low degree.
> He has filled the hungry with good things,
>> and the rich he has sent empty away.

In synthetic parallelism the second stich completes or adds to the thought of the first stich:

> I myself have established my King
>> upon Zion, my holy mountain. (2:6)

> He forgives all your sins,
>> and heals all your diseases.
> He redeems your life from the grave,
>> and crowns you with mercy and love.
> He fills all your years with good,
>> and renews your youth like an eagle's
>>> (103:3-5)

The same form occurs in the antiphon that begins the canticle *Gloria in Excelsis*, Luke 2:14:

> Glory to God in the highest,
>   and peace to his people on earth!

There are many combinations and mutations of these three basic forms of parallelism in the Psalter. A good place to study them is in the nine acrostic Psalms. In these each verse (25, 34, 145), stich (111, 112), or pair of verses (9-10, 37) begins with a letter of the Hebrew alphabet in succession.[7] The *magnum opus* of the acrostic form is Psalm 119. There are twenty-two strophes of eight lines each that progress successively in the order of the twenty-two letters of the alphabet. Each verse in a strophe begins with the same letter. The acrostic pattern was probably designed as an aid to memorization. Most of these Psalms contain moral precepts.[8] But Psalm 145, despite its many quotations from other Psalms, is an effective hymn of praise; and Psalm 119, for all its artificial construction, has remained through the ages a favored meditation for those devoted to the study of God's Word.[9]

There has been much discussion concerning the strophic or stanza arrangement of the Psalms. Modern translations exhibit various schemes of ordering them.[10] Many Psalms seem naturally to fall into related pairs of verses. A few Psalms are obviously composite, such as 19, 24, and 108, which combine poems of independent origin and date. Several of them have retained in their text refrains that mark off the strophic pattern, such as 42-43, 46, 67, 80, and 107.[11] In some cases, strophic structure can be detected by a shift in the person or persons who are addressed (e.g., Psalm 2, with four strophes of three verses each), or by a change from solo to choral parts, as in processional hymns such as Psalms 118 and 132.

In Hebrew poetry each verse contains a complete thought or statement. There are no incomplete lines that have to be carried over to the next verse to round out the sense. For this reason the Psalms lend themselves to a recitation or song rendered antiphonally by verses, or with antiphons or responsive refrains inserted after each verse or group of verses. Except where glosses or corruptions have disturbed the text, the meter is regular, although the same Psalm may exhibit a variety of metric patterns. There is no "metrical foot," however, as in our western poetry and hymnody, either by accent or by units of long and short syllables. Rhythm is achieved by the natural stress or "tone" of the principal words of the line. In any stich there will not be more than four or less than two such words.

Our knowledge of ancient Hebrew pronunciation is scanty. Hence there is often disagreement among scholars regarding the exact rhythmic pattern of many verses. The most common stresses are $3 + 3$ and $3 + 2$, or in verses of three stichs $3 + 2 + 2$ or $2 + 2 + 2$. In some verses it is possible to scan $4 + 4$ or $4 + 3$ or $2 + 2$. In any case, the feel of this rhythm is often possible in English translation, provided that stressed syllables are not accented:

$3 + 3$ Let us *come* before his *pres*ence with thanks*giv*ing,

and *raise* a loud *shout* to him in *psalms.*
(95:2)

3 + 2   Out of the *depths* have I *called* to you,
Lord;
   hear, LORD, my *voice.* (130:1)

2 + 2   The *Lord* is my *shepherd;*
   *noth*ing can I *want.* (23:1)

2. Types of Hebrew Psalms

In the past it was common to study the Psalms either as a liturgical hymn-book or as an anthology of religious verse. Either way, the approach to the Psalter was in terms of a collection of literary texts, composed by authors, whether identifiable or not, who reflected upon the religious needs and experiences of themselves or of their people in various times and circumstances of their lives. Much attention was devoted to the dating of the Psalms—pre-exilic, exilic, or post-exilic—and their literary and theological relationships to datable historical, prophetic, and wisdom materials in other books of the Old Testament.[12] A reference to the Temple, for example, raised the question whether the sanctuary was the first (pre-exilic) or the second (post-exilic) one. Another preoccupation had to do with Psalms in the first person singular—whether the "I" of the Psalms was an individual speaking of his own experience, or a collective or corporate symbol of the people as a whole.[13]

The difficulty with this approach is that it largely overlooks the fact that the Psalms, no less than many narratives, oracles, and aphorisms in the Old Testament, were transmitted orally for many generations, before they were crystallized in written form. That is to say, they were sung and prayed long before they were transcribed. Even then, many of them probably passed through various editorial recensions and collections before they reached the form in which we know them.

Modern critical study of the Psalter accepts the oral, pre-literary transmission of the Psalms, and focuses upon two special interests: 1) analysis and classification of the literary types or patterns of Hebrew poetry; and 2) the distinction between Psalms of a cultic or of a non-cultic origin. The two quests are not mutually exclusive. Most introductions to and commentaries upon the Psalter today make use of the analysis of the German scholar Hermann Gunkel (1862-1932), who distinguished the forms or types *(Gattungen)* of songs, sayings, and narratives, as they developed from communal or folk tradition. He concluded that most of the Psalms originated in communal happenings or individual experiences, especially at the cultic shrines and centers.[14]

The Psalms may be categorized in three basic types: Praise, Lament (or Entreaty), and Instruction. Within each type there are special groupings, or Psalms for particular occasions, whether communal or individual. Many Psalms show mixed types, so that there is no hard and fast line of classification. The following outline is neither detailed nor exhaustive, but is designed to give principal examples of the basic types:

A. PRAISE.

1. *Hymns.* These are essentially liturgical in character. They usually begin, though not always, with an invitation to praise. Then follows the reason for praise, which may be God's wonders in creation and nature or in the history of his people. Sometimes they end with a repetition of the invitation or with a doxology. Examples: 8, 19:1-6, 29, 33, 96, 98, 104, 105, 113, 114, 117, 135, 136, 145-150.

2. *Thanksgivings.* Similar in structure to the Hymns, they may be communal or individual. The occasions refer to a specific aid or help: a good harvest, deliverance from danger or distress, special divine favors:
Examples: Communal, 33, 65, 66, 67, 124, 129; Individual, 18, 21, 22:22-31, 30, 32, 40:1-11, 66, 92, 103, 116, 118, 138.

3. *Songs of Zion.* These hymns celebrate the holy city of Jerusalem, and include songs of pilgrimage to it:[15]
Examples: 46, 48, 87, 122, 134; Pilgrimage, 24:1-6, 84, 125.

B. LAMENT (ENTREATY)

4. *Communal Laments.* These are prayers of complaint and petition, arising from some national catastrophe or defeat, such as the destruction of Jerusalem. They invoke God's help, recall his aid in the past, and normally express confidence in his answer to the plea.
Examples: 44, 60, 74, 79, 80, 83, 85, 89, 106, 123, 126, 137.

5. *Individual Laments.* This is the largest single category in the Psalter. In structure, they are similar to the communal laments, but show a variety of circumstances of petition: sickness, imminent death, persecution, exile, shame and abuse. Most of them also express hope and faith in God's deliverance and execution of justice:

Examples: 3, 5, 6, 7, 13, 17, 22:1-21, 25, 27, 28, 31, 35, 38, 42-43, 51, 54, 55, 56, 57, 58, 59, 63, 64, 69, 70, 71, 86, 88, 102, 109, 120, 130, 139, 140, 141, 142, 143.

6. *Songs of Confidence.* Some Psalms of "lament" are almost entirely given over to expressions of trust and confidence:

Examples: 4, 11, 16, 23, 62, 121, 123, 131.

C. INSTRUCTION

7. *Didactic Psalms.* These Psalms are related to the "wisdom" literature of the Old Testament, and probably were not intended for liturgical use. They denote the way of life of the righteous and the wicked, promote and cultivate devotion to the Law. Many of them are of acrostic form (see Section 1 above). Some also have the character of thanksgiving or lamentation Psalms:

Examples: 1, 14=53, 15, 25, 32, 34, 37, 49, 52, 73, 75, 94, 111, 112, 119, 127, 128. Also 19:7-14, 78, 107.

There are certain groups of Psalms of varied types that reveal a special cultic setting. One of these may be called Processional Liturgies. For example, Psalm 68 is a collection of songs for a procession to the Temple, after a great military victory. It begins with the ancient battle cry that preceded the moving of the Ark in ancient times (cf. Numbers 10:35):

> Let God arise! Let his enemies be scattered!
> Let those who hate him flee before him!

The order of the procession is described (verse 25-27):

> The singers go first,
>   the instrumental players last;
> In the middle are the maidens,
>   playing the timbrels.
> Benjamin, the smallest tribe, leads;
>   the princes of Judah in the throng,
>   the princes of Zebulon and Naphtali.

The scenario recalls the story in 2 Samuel 6-7 of David's bringing of the Ark to Jerusalem, and his hope of building a suitable sanctuary for it on Mount Zion. Psalm 132 may well be a processional hymn for such an anniversary. Some scholars believe that Psalm 24:7-10 was composed for the same event, and that Psalm 18 (= 2 Samuel 22) may be related to it. Other processional Psalms are possibly 95 and 100— invitatory hymns of praise; and certainly Psalm 118, which celebrates a victory of a warrior, and the procession of triumph to the Temple sanctuary.

Another category is the group known as Royal Psalms, in which the king is either the subject or the object of cultic observance. These also are of various

types: prayers by the king, 20, 28, 61, 63, 144; thanksgivings, 18, 21; and a "moral code," 101. Psalm 72 is
a prayer for the king at his accession or coronation,
and Psalms 2 and 110 are oracular utterances for a
similar occasion; Psalm 45 is composed for a royal
wedding. We have already noted Psalm 132 as a
liturgy of royal import; so also may be Psalm 89, a
lament for the downfall of the Judaean monarchy.
These royal Psalms were preserved in the post-
exilic period and given a messianic interpretation, in
the hope of restoration of David's line (see Section
6 below).

A younger friend of Gunkel, the Norwegian scholar
Sigmund Mowinckel (1884-1965), and his disciples
developed the theory of cultic origins of the Psalter,
and considered them for the most part the product
of temple personnel.[16] With great ingenuity they
assigned a large number of Psalms to a compre-
hensive New Year festival at the time of the autumn
ingathering of harvest, to which the name commonly
applied has been "The Enthronement of Yahweh." [17]

This festival was described in terms of dramatic
representations of the creation story—of Yahweh's
conflict with the forces of chaos and his victorious
enthronement as supreme ruler of the universe in
"the assembly of the gods." Involved in this ritual
drama, Israel's king, as representative of Yahweh
and of his people, entered into combat with his
enemies and suffered a temporary defeat. In the end
he was rescued by Yahweh; and in a triumphal cere-
mony he celebrated a re-accession to his own throne.
The theory of this festival is still very much de-
bated.[18]

3. The Psalter of the Temple

The Psalter is often described as the "Hymn Book of the Second Temple," the one rebuilt in 520-515 B.C. by those who had returned from exile in Babylonia.[19] This Temple survived until the time of Herod the Great, who began to rebuild it on a more magnificent scale.[20] But it was destroyed by the Romans in A.D. 70, after a four-year war of rebellion by the Jews of Palestine against them. On its site today stands the beautiful Dome of the Rock, built in 691 by the Muslim Abd al-Malik.

Many Psalms were composed in this post-exilic period, but many others were gathered from earlier times. All these were formed into collections, edited, and finally codified in what came to be the canonical 150 Psalms (see Section 5 below). There is no secure evidence, however, that all of these 150 Psalms, particularly those of a didactic form, were used in the Temple services.

In the rites of the Second Temple, the Psalms were sung by choirs of the Levitical tribes. At various places the people responded with praise-shouts of Hallelujah or refrains such as, "For his mercy endures for ever." [21] A rich orchestra accompanied the Psalms; and it is likely that the mysterious word *Selah,* scattered through the psalm-texts, denoted an orchestral interlude or signal for these responses. The Books of Chronicles, written not earlier than 400 B.C., record the organization of these choirs in the times of David and Solomon. It is more likely that these traditions provide us with information about the Second Temple.[22] The names of some of the choir founders, leaders, or singers, are given in the titles of many Psalms and are possibly derived from collections of their respective choir guilds: Asaph (50, 73-83), the Sons of Korah (42-49, 84-85, 87-88), Jeduthun (39, 62, 77), Heman (88) and Ethan (89). Another notation, in fifty-five Psalms, is "For the Director" or Choirmaster.

Seventy-three Psalms, almost half of the Psalter, are ascribed to David, and a few to other ancient worthies. [23] In the Davidic group are thirteen with historical notes concerning the occasion of composition.[24] Most scholars believe that these notes are due to the final editors of the Psalter. On the other hand there are thirty-four Psalms without any title or ascription. These are often called "orphan" Psalms.[25]

The arrangement of the Psalter into five books also gives us some clues to the editing process, even though it throws little light upon the dating of the collections or of the individual Psalms within them. Each book ends with an editorial doxology; the final one, Psalm 150, serves also as a doxology for the entire Psalter. At the end of the second book there is a curious colophon: "The prayers of David, the Son of Jesse, are ended." Two Psalms in the first book are repeated in the second: 14=53 and 40:13-17=70. Psalm 108 of the fifth book combines Psalms 51:1-11 and 60:5-12 of the second.

Book 1: Psalms 1-41
Psalms 1-2 are "orphans"; the rest are ascribed to David, including nineteen for the Director. The name for God is *Yahweh*. We have here the nucleus of a "Davidic Psalter" from the Southern Kingdom.

Book 2: Psalms 42-72
Psalms 42-49 are ascribed to the Sons of Korah, and 50 to Asaph. Psalms 51-65, 68-70 are ascribed to David, and all of this group, except 63, to the Director. 71 is an "orphan," and 72 is ascribed to Solomon. The preferred name for God is *Elohim*, and probably comes from the Northern Kingdom.

Book 3: Psalms 73-89
Psalms 73-83 are ascribed to Asaph, 84-85 and 87-88 to the Sons of Korah, and 89 to Ethan. Only 86 is a "Prayer of David." 75-77, 80-81, 84-85, and 88 are also ascribed to the Director. Both *Elohim and Yahweh* are used. There are no "orphan" Psalms.

Book 4: Psalms 90-106
Except for Psalms 90 ascribed to Moses, and 101 and 103 to David, the rest of this group are "orphans."

Book 5: Psalms 107-150
Psalms 108-110, 122, 124, 131, 133, and 138-145 are ascribed to David, Psalm 127 to Solomon, and Psalms 109, 139-140 to the Director. The

rest are "orphans." But Psalms 120-134 are entitled "Songs of Ascents."

This schedule suggests that the first three books were
probably older in the main, combining collections
from both northern and southern shrines; the last
two books were later, but picked up many Psalms
from earlier collections.

The superscriptions of the Psalms contain very
few notices of liturgical use.[26] Many more, however,
give titles of musical forms, melodies, and instrumental accompaniments. Unfortunately much of this
information is obscure.[27] For none of these melodies
or their orchestral accompaniment have survived. We
know only the names of the instruments, and these
mainly from pictorial representations in the monu-
ments of Israel's neighbors that are still extant. There
were harps and lyres, flutes and pipes, horns and
trumpets, and resounding and clashing cymbals.[28]
Only one of these survives today in its ancient form:
the *shofar,* or ram's horn, a "bugle" signal for gatherings at the great feasts.

The best description that has come down to us
recounting the worship in the Temple is that of the
apocryphal Book of the Wisdom of Jesus the Son of
Sirach (commonly referred to as Ecclesiasticus or
Sirach). It describes the leadership of the high-
priest Simon II (ca. 220-195 B.C.). After noting his
benefits to the people and his gorgeous vestments at
the time of worship, the author proceeds to tell us:

When he put on his glorious robe
    and clothed himself with superb perfection

And went up to the holy altar,
  he made the court of the sanctuary glorious.
And when he received the portions
  from the hands of the priests,
As he stood by the hearth of the altar
  with a garland of brethren around him,
He was like a young cedar on Lebanon;
  and they surrounded him like the trunks of palm
    trees,
All the sons of Aaron in their splendor
  with the Lord's offering in their hands,
  before the whole Congregation of Israel.

Finishing the service at the altars,
  and arranging the offering to the Most High,
    the Almighty,
He reached out his hand to the cup
  and poured a libation of the blood of the grape;
He poured it out at the foot of the altar,
  a pleasing odor to the Most High, the King of all.
Then the sons of Aaron shouted,
  they sounded the trumpets of hammered work,
They made a great noise to be heard
  for remembrance before the Most High.

Then all the people made haste
  and fell to the ground upon their faces
  to worship their Lord, the Almighty, God Most
  High.
And the singers praised him with their voice
  in sweet and full-toned melody.
And the people besought the Lord Most High
  in prayer before him who is merciful,

Till the order of worship of the Lord was ended;
  so they completed his service.

Then Simon came down, and lifted up his hands
  over the whole congregation of the sons of Israel,
To pronounce the blessings of the Lord with his
  lips, and to glory in his Name;
And they bowed down in worship a second time,
  to receive the blessing from the Most High.

(Ecclesiasticus 50:11-21)

4. The Psalms in Synagogue Worship

Little is known of the time of origin of the synagogue institution, and many theories have been proposed to explain its rise and development.[29] The most common hypothesis is that the synagogue gatherings arose in the time of the Exile after the destruction of the Temple, to keep the Jewish communities in Palestine and in their dispersion in other lands loyal to their faith and constant in devotion to God's Law.[30] There are archaeological finds referring to synagogues in Egypt from the middle of the third century B.C. But the earliest literary references to them are from early Christian times, in the writings of the New Testament and in those of the Jewish philosopher Philo of Alexandria (d. after A.D. 40) and the Jewish historian Josephus (d. early second century). In all three sources the synagogue is considered an ancient institution founded by Moses.[31]

The synagogue served many purposes in the life of a Jewish community. On Sabbaths and other holy days it was the gathering place for worship. It was also a schoolhouse, both for the education of children and for study classes of adults; and frequently it was a gathering place for interests of the Jewish community other than religious. Many synagogues had hostels for travelers and pilgrims. Ever since the destruction of the last Jerusalem Temple in A.D. 70, the synagogue has remained the principal religious institution of Judaism.

We know the basic elements of synagogue services of worship in early Christian times. They consisted of the recital of the *Shema*, the "confession" of Jewish faith [32]; readings in sequential course from the books of the Law, followed by selected readings from the Prophets, with interpretations and homilies upon these lessons; and benedictions and prayers addressed to God. If a priest were present, he was invited to give the Blessing pronounced in the Temple services. [33]

Many of the prayers contained phrases from the Psalms; but the introduction of Psalm singing in synagogue worship is a matter of dispute. Some authorities believe that from early times Psalms appointed for certain days and festivals in the Temple services were used in the synagogue, and from this custom the use of psalmody in the services of the early Christians was derived. Others believe that psalmody in Christian worship ante-dated its introduction in the synagogue. There are both similarities and dissimilarities in the use of Psalms in the liturgies of synagogue and church: [34]

Similarities:

1. The Psalms were sung by cantors, interspersed with refrains or responses by the people, not by choirs such as those of the Temple.
2. The Psalms were not accompanied by any in-

struments. Both synagogue and church authorities considered the use of instruments "unspiritual" and associated with pagan worship.

3. The patterns of monotone recitation with inflections and cadences, according to the sense of the text, with certain festal jubilations (as in the "Alleluia") for chanting either lessons or Psalms.

Dissimilarities:

4. The use of Psalms between the lessons, characteristic of all Christian liturgies, but unknown in the synagogue before the eighth century.

5. The regular course recitation or singing of the Psalms in their entirety in the Christian Daily Offices, and in some seasons of the Church Year, in certain Psalms appointed in the Eucharist. In Jewish worship, both in Temple and synagogue, not all of the Psalms were used, and never were they appointed in sequential course, other than the Hallel Psalms at the great festivals (113-118).

Much research in modern times has been given to recording and transcribing the synagogue music of Jewish communities which through the centuries have been isolated from Western influence. The Jews in the Trans-Caucasia and in Yemen particularly have yielded melodic patterns in fairly defined modes that have many similarities to the most ancient chants of the church, whether Byzantine, Ambrosian, or Gregorian. The conclusions reached suggest that there is some continuity of song between the synagogue and the church, even though borrowing of specific tunes from one to the other cannot be precisely demonstrated.[35]

5. New Psalms in Late Judaism and the Early Church

The Hebrew Bible used by the Jews, which Christians call the Old Testament, has three major divisions: the Law, the Prophets, and the Writings. The Law (Genesis-Deuteronomy) was canonized, *i.e.*, accepted as divine revelation not later than the time of Ezra, *ca.* 444 B.C. The Prophets were not finally edited and canonized before the end of the third century B.C.[36] The other books, the Writings, received their final canonization about A.D. 90, though the Psalter, included in this third division, was undoubtedly accepted at a much earlier time.

The Wisdom of Sirach (Ecclesiasticus), dating from about 180 B.C., has a long synopsis in chapters 44-49 of canonical Scripture that included at least a Davidic Psalter (47:8-10). The first Book of Maccabees, written a century later, quotes Psalm 79:2-3 as Scripture. In the Gospel of Luke, our Lord refers (24:44) to the Law, the Prophets, and the Psalms.

This data suggests that the completion of a canonical book of 150 Psalms had evolved not later than

100 B.C. This dating does not exclude later editorial revisions. It explains the variations of the ancient Greek version from that of the Hebrew in enumeration of the Psalms, [37] additional superscriptions, and the inclusion of an additional Psalm 151. It also leaves room for revisions, if not new compositions, of certain Psalms in the "Maccabean" period.[38]

Of special interest is the incomplete scroll of the Psalms discovered in 1956 in Cave 11 at Qumran, [39] where the sectarian Essene community settled ca. 165-150 B.C. The manuscript, however, dates from approximately A.D. 30-50, and includes all or parts of 39 canonical Psalms in an unusual order, interspersed with "the last words of David" (2 Samuel 23:1-7) and eight apocryphal Psalms that include Sirach 51:13 ff. and the additional Psalm 151 of the Greek version.[40] Some of the texts have interesting variants, and Psalm 145 has after each verse a refrain:

> Blessed be the LORD,
> and blessed be his Name for ever and ever.

The Qumran community also produced many original Psalms of their own composition. One of the scrolls contains a collection of hymns, and the *Manual of Discipline* scroll concludes with a lengthy hymn, including such lines as these:

> I will meditate on his might,
>   and lean on his mercies every day.
> I know that in his hand is judgment of all living,
>   and that all his works are truth.
> I will praise him when distress is unleashed,
>   and will shout for joy for his salvation.[41]

Other Jewish Psalms from the pre-Christian era include the well-known *Song of the Three Young Men* in the apocryphal additions to the Book of Daniel. The Song is an expanded version of Psalm 148. A collection of eighteen *Psalms of Solomon* is extant in a Greek translation of an original Hebrew text. They are messianic in theme, and emanate from Pharisaic circles in the middle of the first century B.C., when the Romans took control of Palestine and deposed the Hasmonean prince of Judah.

The continuing production of new psalmody was taken up in the early Christian communities, and was a constituent part of their worship (see Section 7 below). In fact, many of the sayings of Jesus preserved in the Gospels are in poetic form, [42] notably the Beatitudes and much of the discourses in John. Of the many early Christian Psalms and hymns scattered through the New Testament, those of Luke 1-2 have found a permanent place in the liturgies of the church: the *Magnificat, Benedictus, Gloria in Excelsis,* and *Nunc Dimittis.* In recent experimental services many of the "anthems" of the book of Revelation have come into use. [43] Hymns cited by St. Paul in Philippians 2:6-11 and Colossians 1:15-20, have a more Hellenistic form; but the prolog of the Gospel of John utilizes a hymn with the Semitic "parallelism of verse members" of synthetic form:

> In the beginning was the Word,
>   and the Word was with God,
> And the Word was God;
>   he was in the beginning with God.

II.

Psalmody in
the Church's Liturgy

6. The Psalms: A Prophecy of Christ

In the New Testament there are 93 quotations from more than 60 of the Psalms.[44] Among the sayings of Jesus in the Gospels there are more quotations from the Psalter than from any other book of the Old Testament. The evangelists added many more, as proof texts of his fulfillment of prophecy, in his baptism and temptation, his ministry and teaching, and especially in his passion. Jesus' last recorded parable, that of the wicked tenants in the vineyard, includes a summary interpretation taken from Psalm 118:22:[45]

> The stone that the builders rejected
> has become the chief cornerstone.

In his final commission to his disciples after his resurrection, according to St. Luke, he said: "everything written about me in the law of Moses and the prophets and the psalms must be fulfilled" (24:44).

St. Peter in his sermon at the church's first Pentecost, in addition to his text from the prophet Joel, cited also Psalms 16, 132, and 110, from David, who is called "a prophet," foretelling Christ's resurrection and ascension.[46] Similarly, in St. Paul's first recorded sermon, at Antioch of Pisidia, citations from Psalms 89, 2, and 16, are interspersed with texts from the prophets Isaiah and Habakkuk.[47] The letters of both St. Peter and St. Paul quote the Psalms frequently in didactic as well as prophetic contexts.[48] The author of the Letter to the Hebrews is particularly fond of texts from the Psalms in support of his doctrines of Christ's incarnation, ascension, and eternal priesthood.[49] The seer of Revelation weaves many allusions to the Psalter into his anthems, notably those from the Hallel Psalms (113-118) in the paean of invitation to the marriage Supper of the Lamb. [50]

For the early Christians the Psalter was "David's Prophecy" of the One who fulfilled God's promise to him:

> I will raise up your son after you,
>   who shall come forth from your body,
>   and I will establish his kingdom.
> He shall build a house for my Name,
>   and I will establish the throne
>   of his kingdom for ever.
> I will be his father,
>   and he shall be my son.[51]

Thus all the "Royal Psalms," which in late Judaism were given a messianic interpretation, were applied to Christ, the son of David no less than Son of God. So Jesus was hailed at his triumphal entry into Jerusalem, with an acclamation from Psalm 118:26 which has become a constituent anthem of the church's liturgy since ancient times:

> Hosanna!
> Blessed is he who comes
>   in the Name of the Lord!
> Blessed be the kingdom
>   of our father David
>   that is coming!
> Hosanna in the highest! [52]

Likewise his anguish in Gethsemane and his agony
on Calvary gathered up all the laments of the Psalter.
The Passion narratives of the Gospels are replete
with references to them, especially to Psalms 22 and
69; for example,

> All who see me deride and make sport of me,
>   curling their lips and tossing their heads:
> "He trusted in the LORD; let him save him!
>   Let him rescue him, if he delights in him!"

> I looked for sympathy and for comforters;
>   but I could find none.
> They put bitter gall in my food,
>   and gave me vinegar for my thirst.[53]

Just as Christ fulfilled the ideals of kingship in the
Psalter and experienced to the full the sufferings of
the faithful and righteous servant of God, so also
the fortunes of Israel, both good and ill, are trans-
ferred to the "new Israel," the church, the chosen
and elect in Christ. The enemies of Israel are identi-
fied with the persecutors of the church, or, by alle-
gorical exegesis, with its spiritual foes within and
without who assault and test its faith and hope:

> For your sake we are killed all the day long;
>   we are accounted as sheep for the slaughter.[54]

The Psalms foretold, as did the later prophets, the universal mission of the church among the Gentiles.[55] St. Paul made an unusual application of Psalm 19:4, among passages from Isaiah, regarding the preaching of the apostles:

> Their sound is gone out into all lands,
>   and their words to the end of the world.[56]

In similar vein, the devotion of the psalmists to the city of Jerusalem and its Temple was related to Christ and the church,[57] or to "the holy city, new Jerusalem, coming down out of heaven from God," where there is "no temple in the city, for its temple is the Lord God the Almighty and the Lamb."[58]

This prophetic interpretation of the Psalter in the New Testament is the key to the church's use of the Psalms in the liturgy. It has been called the "Christologizing" of the Psalter. Every psalm is thus understood as an address between the Father and the Son, or between the church and its God or its Redeemer. Although this understanding of the Psalter's praises and prayers separates Christians from Jews in their common hymnal, yet in a deeper sense they are at one, for both sing and pray the Psalms in faith and hope in God's promises of ever larger fulfillments.

7. Responsorial Psalmody: The Gradual

The New Testament writings do not provide us with a liturgy of the early Christians, though they do refer to the constituent elements of their worship: teaching and preaching, prayer, praise, and sharing in "the breaking of bread." [59] St. Paul mentioned the "spiritual gifts" *(charismata)* that individual members shared with one another in worship: a psalm, a lesson, a prophecy, a speaking in tongues with its interpretation.[60] Elsewhere he referred to "psalms, hymns, and spiritual songs." [61] Some of these early hymns and psalms we have already noted (above, section 5) found a place in the New Testament.

Our earliest description of the Sunday liturgy of the church is related by Justin, a teacher and apologist in the church at Rome in the middle of the second century:

> When all who live in the city and the country have come together, the memoirs of the apostles and the writings of the prophets are read, as long as there is time. After the reader has finished, the president instructs

and exhorts us to imitate these excellent things. Then we stand together and offer our prayers; and when we have ended these, bread and wine and water are brought forward. The president, likewise, now offers prayers and thanksgivings, according to his ability, and the people assent with *Amen.* Each one then receives and shares in the elements over which thanksgiving has been offered; and a portion is sent to those who are absent by the deacons.[62]

Justin does not specifically mention psalm-singing. He may have included it in his reference to "the writings of the prophets"; for in his extant apologetic works he considered the Psalter a prophetic book. His outline is confirmed, with special mention of psalmody, a half-century later by an early Church Father of North Africa named Tertullian: "the Scriptures are read and the Psalms are sung, sermons are delivered and petitions are offered." [63]

The oldest liturgies of the Church, in both the East and West, appoint at least three lessons: from the Old Testament, from the Epistles or Acts, and from the Gospels. After the Old Testament lesson a psalm was sung, and after the Epistle, an Alleluia chant. At a later time, when the lessons were normally reduced to two, the Psalm and the Alleluia were sung consecutively after the first lesson. In the Latin Church this psalm came to be called the "Gradual" because it was sung from the step (*gradus*) of the ambo or pulpit where the lesson was read or intoned.[64]

The Gradual is the earliest form of psalmody we can trace in the Eucharist. It was chanted by a cantor, with a refrain by the congregation, or later by the choir. It may be considered as an added, prophetic Old Testament lesson.[65] There is no evidence from the early period of the church of any fixed schedule or table of lessons and psalms. The president of the liturgical assembly chose whatever selections he desired. But there is one link, however, between Jewish and Christian usage that goes back to very ancient times: namely, the singing of the Hallel Psalms (113-118) at the Jewish Passover and the Christian *Pascha* or Easter. In the liturgies of both the Eastern and Western Churches, Psalm 118 was appointed for Easter Day, with its refrain from verse 24:

> This is the day when the LORD has acted;
> let us rejoice and be glad in it! [66]

The form of the Gradual is that of a responsorial psalm. That is to say, a cantor or cantors sang the text of the psalm and the people responded after each verse or group of verses with a fixed refrain. The model for this form, if not taken over by the church directly from Jewish usage, could be deduced from many of the Psalms themselves. Many of them contain recurring refrains [67] or the praise-shout of "Hallelujah" (or *Alleluia* as transcribed in the ancient versions in Greek and Latin).[68] One of our earliest references to the form is from St. Athanasius of Alexandria (d. 373): "I sat down on my throne and requested the deacon to read a psalm, and the people to answer, 'For his steadfast love endures for ever.' " [69]

Originally the music of the Gradual was very simple, as were the chants of the lessons. St. Augustine (d. 431) recalled a tradition that St. Athanasius "had the reader of the Psalm utter it with so slight a modulation of the voice, that he seemed to be speaking it rather than singing it." [70] In his own day the melodies of the Gradual had become more elaborate, for they were now the song of more professional soloists. At a synod of Rome in 595, Pope Gregory the Great (d. 604) directed that the Gradual no longer be assigned to the deacon, but to lesser ministries:

> A very reprehensible custom has for some time existed, that certain singers are selected for the ministry of the altar, who, being ordained deacons, devote themselves to singing, instead of to their proper duties of preaching and almsgiving. The result frequently is that while search is made for a good voice, no care is taken to provide that the life shall be such as harmonizes with the holy ministry. And so the singer enrages God by his conduct, while he delights the people with his accents. [71]

8. Antiphonal Psalmody:
The Introit, Offertory, and Communion

After the conversion to Christianity of the Emperor Constantine in 312, the church had peace from persecution. Benefactions from the emperors and other wealthy Christians made possible the building of handsome churches and a more splendid public liturgy. The simpler music of the church's worship in the age of persecution was now developed, with the organization of choirs, to supplement the congregational responses to the melodies of the cantors. In this context we learn of a new style of psalmody: antiphonal singing, i.e., the singing of the verses of the Psalms alternately by two groups of singers.

The custom began in Antioch in the mid-fourth century. To counter the hymns and songs of the Arian heretics, then favored by the bishop of the city, two devout laymen, Flavian and Diodore—who later became bishops, the one of Antioch and the other of Tarsus—began to teach the Orthodox Christians, in their vigils at the shrines of the martyrs, to form two groups and "to sing the Psalms of David antiphonally." [72] The new style of psalmody spread rapidly among monastic communities (below, section 12), and to the vigils of other churches. St. John Chrysostom (d. 407), an Antiochene, began its use while Bishop of Constantinople; [73] and St. Ambrose (d. 397) introduced it to the Western Church in his see of Milan.[74]

In a letter to his clergy of Caesarea (modern Kaysari, Turkey), St. Basil (d. 379), himself a noted monastic founder, defended the new custom of antiphonal psalmody at the vigils of his people. He distinguishes clearly the two methods: antiphonal and responsorial.

> The customs now in vogue are in harmony and accord with all the churches of God. For among us the people rise early at night to go to the house of prayer, and in labour and affliction and continuous tears confessing to God, finally rise from their prayers and enter upon the singing of psalms. And now indeed divided into two groups they sing antiphonally, thereby both strengthening their practice in reciting the Scriptures and securing both their close attention and means of keeping their hearts from distraction.

> Then again after entrusting to one person to lead the chant, the rest sing the response; and so having passed the night in a variety of psalm-singing, and praying in the meantime, as the day begins to dawn all in common, as of one voice and one

heart, intone the psalm of confession [Psalm 51] to the Lord.[75]

At Rome antiphonal psalmody was introduced into the liturgy of the Eucharist sometime in the fifth century.[76] An ancient tradition ascribed the origin of the Introit psalm to Pope Celestine I (422-432). About the same time antiphonal psalmody at the Offertory and the Communion came into use.[77] It is not certain whether these psalms were sung by all the people, or in certain of the larger basilicas by monastic communities founded next to them in part for this purpose.[78] By the sixth century, at least, these antiphonal psalms had been entrusted to the papal choir school *(schola cantorum)* of men and boys.[79]

In the early church, as in the Jewish synagogue, the songs and chants of the liturgy were unaccompanied by any instruments. Hence the psalmody required a cantor to set the melody and mode of the psalm to be sung. At first, the leader of song would chant the first line of the psalm so that all would know its melodic setting. But with the development of choirs and more skilled singers a new introduction to the psalmody came into use, namely, the "antiphon." One or two verses of the psalm, or in some cases a verse taken from another book of Scripture, would be sung before the psalm and at its conclusion as a thematic frame, as well as a melodic one. The choice of antiphons was determined more and more in response to the developing feasts and seasons of the Church Year, so that its thematic relevance was enhanced. By changing the antiphon the same psalm might be used in more than one season.[80] Since the antiphon was sung by a cantor, its music tended to become more elaborate, just as the psalm sung for the Gradual (above, section 7).

Another characteristic of antiphonal psalmody was the use of a doxology, the *Gloria Patri*, at the end of the psalm. Its origins go back to the beginnings of antiphonal psalmody at Antioch. Though its purpose was to give a Christian ending to the Psalms, its earliest forms were a matter of dispute with the Arian heretics, who preferred, "Glory to the Father through the Son in the Holy Spirit." In order to stress the equality of the three Persons of the Trinity the orthodox form in the Eastern Churches came to be:

> Glory to the Father and to the Son
>   and to the Holy Spirit,
> Now and always and to the ages of ages.

To emphasize the eternity of the three Persons, again in opposition to the Arians, the Western Churches added to the second part of the *Gloria:* "As it was in the beginning." [81]

9. Changes in Form

The three antiphonal Psalms in the ancient liturgy of the church in Rome were intended as devotional accompaniments to processions within the rite. The Introit was sung during the entrance of the ministers from the sacristy to their places within the sanctuary. The Offertory and Communion Psalms covered the processions of the people to a place near the altar, where they brought their gifts and later came forward to receive communion. They were sung as long as needed to cover these processions. If the procession was completed before the Psalm was finished, the celebrant gave a signal to the leader of the choir to proceed at once to the *Gloria Patri*. It was not necessary to prolong the chant beyond the time required for the liturgical ceremonies.

The Gradual Psalm was a more integral part of the rite, whether viewed as an additional prophetic lesson or as a bridge between the Old Testament lesson and the Epistle. In later times, when the Old Testament lesson was normally omitted, leaving only the Epistle and Gospel, the Gradual was sung immediately before the Alleluia, between the Epistle and the Gospel. Hence the Gradual with the Alleluia also came to be an accompaniment to a procession—that of the deacon to the ambo or pulpit from which he intoned the Gospel lesson.

As long as these processions continued to be an integral part of the liturgy, the psalm chants continued to be sung in full, or in part as needed, with their antiphons and responses. In the course of the Middle Ages, at various times and places, these processions became very attenuated in length. Frequency of communion by the people was limited to a few times or only once a year. Hence the Offertory and Communion processions gradually disappeared, except in cathedrals, and the larger collegiate and monastic churches. In most parish churches there were only one or two resident clergy, and so the Introit and Gospel processions also became in the course of time very much reduced in length. In few of these churches was there anything comparable to a choir, or even cantors, who could read the Latin of the services or manage the liturgical chant of the psalmody. The end result of this development in the later Middle Ages was the reduction of the psalmody to a few verses usually read by the priest.[82]

Another factor was the scarcity and cost of books. Before the invention of printing, much less of copying machines and cheap paper, books were very expensive, as they were copied by hand usually on parchment. In the earlier centuries, the leaders of worship each had a manuscript of only those parts of the liturgy for which they were responsible. The priest had his *sacramentary* or prayer-book, the readers had their lectionaries, and the singers their chant books. In a medieval parish such a collection of books was neither practical nor economically feasible. Thus all of the parts of the liturgy came to be copied in one volume, the *Missal*, for the convenience of the priests who had to read or sing the prayers, lessons, and chants. The people's parts consisted of brief responses which they would know by heart. There were no service-books available to them, even if they could have been able to read them. To save space, and thus cost, formularies were shortened; and those which occurred regularly, such as the *Gloria Patri*, were abbreviated.

The antiphonal psalmody of the liturgy preserved its basic form only in the Introit. Its final structure consisted of antiphon, one or at most two verses of the Psalm, the *Gloria*, and the antiphon repeated at the end. The Offertory Psalm, at an early stage was changed from an antiphonal to a responsorial form; but in the end it was reduced simply to the antiphon (or response) with occasionally a verse of the Psalms. Communion chants, originally designed to cover the communion of the people, now became only a single verse, usually the antiphon taken as often as not from other Scriptural sources than the Psalms. It was often a "post-communion" said by the priest, since normally only the celebrant communicated.

The Gradual Psalm also suffered a similar diminution. It consisted only of the response and one or two Psalm verses, followed by the Alleluia with its text of Scripture usually selected from books other than the Psalms. Only in Lent, when the Alleluia was omitted, was a portion of the Psalms sung or said after the Gradual. This was known at the Tract, from the Latin *tractim* ("straight through"), since it was sung without antiphon or response. On the First Sunday of Lent the Tract consisted of the entire 91st Psalm, and on Palm Sunday most of Psalm 22.

The survival of the rich melodic corpus of Gregorian plain chant is little short of miraculous, since for several centuries it was taught through an oral tradition. Only in the ninth century did any pattern of musical notation develop, the *neumes,* which at first consisted of signs denoting melodic figure but not pitch or rhythm.[83] By the year 1200 these signs had developed into the square-shaped forms that are still found in many liturgical chant books today. In general, Psalm verses, except in the Gradual, were set to simple melodic cadences; but the antiphons and responsorial Psalms had more florid and melismatic melodies, especially the *jubilus* of the Alleluias.

The introduction of the Roman rite and its chant by Charlemagne (d. 814) to the churches of northern Europe presented a musical problem to these Germanic people who found the liquid and mellifluous chants of a Mediterranean culture difficult to memorize or sing. In order to cope with this problem, the practice was invented—probably at St. Gall —of inserting for mnemonic purposes pious texts within the chants, so that to each note there was a syllable. These unofficial texts were called "tropes." [84] In particular, the florid *jubilus* of the Alleluias were troped with what developed into hymns known as Sequences, which in time took on metrical forms and an independent pursuit of composition. The tropes and most of the Sequence hymns were swept away during the Reformation.[85]

10. Reformation Adaptations

Reform of the liturgy was a basic concern of the Western Church in the sixteenth century, not only in the Protestant churches that broke away from Rome but also in the Roman Catholic Church itself. The official *Missal* promulgated by Pope Pius V in 1570 removed many devotional accretions of medieval times. For example, only four Sequence hymns were retained—those of Easter, Pentecost, Corpus Christi, and the *Dies irae* of the Requiem Mass. On the other hand, the truncated psalmody of the Mass that developed in the Middle Ages was affirmed. Only in the recent reform of the Roman rite since the Second Vatican Council has a serious review of psalmody in the Mass been undertaken (see Section 16 below).

Luther's approach to psalmody in the Eucharist was conservative since he wished to keep whatever was Scriptural in the old Latin rites. In his revised Latin Mass *(Formula Missae et Communionis)* for the church in Wittenberg, issued in 1523, he retained the Introits, Graduals, Alleluias, and Communions, but repudiated everything connected with the Offer-

tory since, as he said, it "sounds and reeks of obla-
tion." He would have preferred to restore a full
Psalm for the Introit, but settled for "the received
usage." He kept the short Gradual but disliked the
Tract in Lent as "tedious."

Pressure for the vernacular, however, and experi-
ments with it of which he disapproved led Luther
to produce his outline of a German Mass (*Deutsche
Messe und Ordnung Gottesdienst*) in 1526. For the
Introit he proposed the use of a vernacular hymn or
a Psalm in German to the simple Gregorian Tone I.
The Gradual was replaced by a German hymn sung
by the choir. There was, of course, no Offertory, but
at the Communion he suggested several German
hymns or a vernacular *Agnus Dei*. There was no
mention of the Alleluia chant.

Luther was neither an iconoclast nor a legalist
with respect to liturgy. He made no claim to a
definitive reconstruction of the church's worship.
His interests were mainly theological and pastoral.
He had no objection to the continued use of Latin
where it was taught and understood; hence he did
not consider his German Mass to be universally appli-
cable. It was designed primarily for "the unedu-
cated laity" in places where "there were no capable
choirs." [86] The Church Orders (*Kirchenordnungen*)
of the various Lutheran states of Germany and
Scandinavia followed in the main the outlines of
Luther's Latin or German Masses or a mixture of
the two. A number of musical editions of liturgical
texts, called *Cantionales*, whether encouraged or inspired by Luther, appeared on through the sixteenth
century. These provided both Latin and adapted

vernacular settings of the propers of the liturgy. The decline of this rich musical culture of both traditional and contemporary design only set in with the disruptions of the Thirty Years' War of 1618-1648.

The reforms led by Zwingli and Calvin in Switzerland were more radically innovative. Though he himself was an accomplished musician, Zwingli banned all music, instrumental and vocal, from his vernacular rite of the Lord's Supper. Calvin, on the other hand, promoted psalm-singing—albeit in metrical forms—as the one legitimate song that conformed to scriptural models of worship. Since the Church Year was largely abandoned in the Calvinistic churches, there was little regard for the traditional assignments of Psalms to days and seasons, or to any particular service of worship.

The completed French Psalter of 1562, published in Geneva, was a notable achievement both in its literary and musical qualities, especially the varieties of poetic meters and melodic rhythms.[87] Forty-nine of the Psalms were translated by Clément Marot, sometime courtier of King Francis I at Paris, who worked with Calvin at Geneva for a year not long before his death in 1544. The rest of the translations were by Theodore Beza (d. 1605), Calvin's associate and successor. The melodies were composed by Louis Bourgeois (d. after 1561).[88] Not only Bourgeois, but other distinguished French composers, such as Claude Goudimel and Claudin Le Jeune, published harmonic and polyphonic arrangements of the melodies. This Psalter has been translated into twenty languages—the earliest being those in Dutch (1566) and German (1573).

In the First Prayer Book of 1549 of the Church of England, Archbishop Cranmer provided an Introit Psalm for all the propers of the Holy Communion. Except for the Christmas season, and a few days of Lent and Eastertide, these followed a basically sequential course. No provision was made for a Gradual, Offertory or Communion Psalm. In the Second Prayer Book of 1552 the Introit Psalm disappeared, and with it all psalmody at the Eucharist until the restorations of recent times. There is no explanation of this. It is generally thought that since Cranmer provided for a full round of psalmody at the Daily Offices (see Section 15 below), including days when the Holy Communion followed immediately after Morning Prayer, he considered that sufficient psalmody was included in the public services.

The strong Puritan elements that developed in the English Reformation were much enamoured with Calvin's work at Geneva. Many of the exiles there during Queen Mary's reign (1554-1559) drank of the stream of metrical psalmody. At Geneva they produced a metrical version in English of fifty-one Psalms. But the entire Psalter in English metric verse that became most popular was that published in London in 1562 by John Day, often called the "Old Version" or "Sternhold and Hopkins" (from some of the principal versifiers), and provided with sixty-five tunes drawn from German and French sources. From this beginning, many harmonized tunes for these Psalms were produced, many of them of a stately dignity, some of which survive in modern hymnals, including others from Scottish metrical Psalters. The quality of the texts, however, left much to be desired, despite their long popularity on into the 18th century.[89]

Metrical psalmody was never officially recognized in the early Prayer Books, or indeed any other hymns. Queen Elizabeth I, in her Injunctions of 1559, allowed their use only under the following conditions:

> And that there be a modest and distinct song so used in all parts of the common prayers in the church, that the same may be as plainly understanded, as if it were read without singing; and yet nevertheless for the comforting of such that delight in music, it may be permitted, that in the beginning, or in the end of common prayers, either at morning or evening, there may be sung an hymn, or suchlike song to the praise of Almighty God, in the best sort of melody and music that may be conveniently devised, having respect that the sentence of the hymn may be understanded and perceived.[90]

III.

Psalmody in
the Daily Offices

11. The Origin of the Daily Offices

The Daily Offices have their roots in the custom of pious Jews in the time of our Lord, which was carried over into the devotion of the early Christians. Three times a day, at the hours of the sacrifices in the Temple, early morning, noon, and late afternoon, the devout Jew would face towards Jerusalem and offer prayer.[91] In this way the personal devotions of those distant from Jerusalem was linked in spirit with the daily round of public worship in the holy city.

The Jewish custom continued in the church even after its membership became predominantly Gentile. In fact, the times of daily prayer were increased. By the end of the second century there is evidence of a daily rhythm of prayer that counted six times of pause and reflection. These were not related, as was Jewish practice, to any times of corporate worship;[92] but they were periods of recollection of the saving events of Christ's death and resurrection, and reminders of the Christian's duty to "watch" for the coming of the Lord.[93] In a manual of church order, written about A.D. 200 attributed to the priest Hippolytus of Rome, this six-fold pattern of daily devotion was outlined as follows:

1. *Dawn.* Rise from sleep and pray before going to work.
2. *Third Hour* (9 a.m.). Pray and recall that at this hour Christ was nailed to the Cross.
3. *Sixth Hour* (noon). Pray, for at this hour darkness covered the earth.
4. *Ninth Hour* (3 p.m.), Pray, remembering that the Lord was pierced and died.
5. *Evening.* Pray before one rests in sleep.
6. *Midnight.* Arise and pray, for at this hour the Bridegroom comes (cf. Matthew 25:6; Mark 13:35).

Hippolytus then completes the cycle by a reference to prayer at the cockcrow (i.e., dawn), when prayer recalls both the condemnation of Jesus by the Jewish Sanhedrin and also the hour of the Resurrection.[94] In this cycle every day of prayer is made a re-living in the believer of the redemptive act of Christ.[95]

We have no way of knowing how many Christians followed this discipline of devotion. By the third century there were already many individual ascetics as well as communities of men and women who were under vows of a life of prayer and charitable work. These were the seed-beds of later monastic communities in which the daily offices of prayer were to be shaped. Nor do we know much about the content of these daily devotions. They certainly included the Lord's Prayer and Bible reading and meditation, and possibly also the recital of Psalms.

12. The Psalms in Monastic and Collegial Communities

The Psalter as a vehicle of Christian prayer came into its own in the daily devotions and services of the monks, whether they pursued a solitary existence or lived in communities that observed a rule. Whatever the reasons were for the rapid and widespread development of monasticism, first in the east and then in the west during the fourth century, the monastic vocation was essentially one of prayer. And the Psalms were the basic substance of it. To achieve this ideal, all worldly ties and occupations had to be abandoned, except for what was absolutely necessary for subsistence. The monk viewed his renunciation of the world for the sake of the kingdom of God as an imitation of the life of his Lord. By using the Psalm texts as the basic vehicle of prayer and meditation, the monk also sought to enter into the spirit of the Lord's own prayer.

By the latter part of the fourth century, monastic communities, under the leadership of abbots (in Egypt, "elders"), became more organized for worship in assemblies at stated times. In Egypt there

were two: Vespers and Nocturns. Each service had
twelve Psalms, sung by two or more cantors in turn
while the others sat in low stalls with reverent attention. After each Psalm there was a prayer and period
of silence for meditation. Only at the end of the
whole psalmody did the brothers rise and sing together the *Gloria Patri*. At the conclusion of Nocturns, toward dawn, Psalms 148-150 were sung. In
other places these were considered a separate office
and named "Lauds" or "Matins."

In Palestine and elsewhere in the near east the
monastic communities also observed in common worship the traditional "day hours" of three Psalms each:
Prime, Terce, Sext, and Nones (i.e., 6 and 9 a.m.,
noon, and 3 p.m.). These Psalms were often sung antiphonally. John Cassian, a westerner from Gaul who
visited these Eastern monasteries in the last decade
of the fourth century, related that the hour of Prime
was introduced to prevent the monks from taking
too much rest and sleep between the long night service and the office of Terce.[96] Be that as it may, the
scheme of seven offices of psalmody and prayer was
justified by the verse of Psalm 119:164, "Seven times
a day do I praise you, because of your righteous
judgments." The same sevenfold times of prayer is
ordered in the Longer Rules of St. Basil of Caesarea
in Asia Minor (d. 379), whose ascetical writings were
to become the foundation of all later Eastern monasticism. In fact, Basil had an additional office at bed-
time, which has come to be known as Compline.[97]

Monasteries in the West followed a variety of rules
derived from Eastern models. But the *Rule* of St.
Benedict of Nursia (d. ca. 540), written for his

foundation at Monte Cassino in southern Italy, was ultimately to become the foundation for all religious orders in the West, as St. Basil's was for the East. Benedict's *Rule* shows acquaintance with many earlier rules, including those of Basil and Cassian; but it probably reflects in the main the customs of the monasteries at Rome located near the great basilicas, such as St. Peter's.[98]

Unlike the regulations of St. Basil, the *Rule* of St. Benedict gives specific instruction for the content of the several Daily Offices as to Psalms, lessons, canticles, other devotions. There are eight Offices, counted as seven to accord with Psalm 119:164, since Nocturns and Lauds were sung without any break between them. The Psalms for these Offices are distributed so that all 150 are sung once a week. Certain Psalms are appointed for specific Offices; the others are sung in sequential course. The scheme is as follows:

> *Nocturns.* Psalm 3 and 95 are sung daily as invitatories. Twelve other Psalms follow, taken in course, unless assigned otherwise, from Psalms 21-109.
>
> *Lauds (Matins).* Psalms 67, 51, and at the conclusion, 148-150 sung daily. After Psalm 51, the following are appointed on each day:

Sundays: 118, 63	Thursdays: 88, 90
Mondays: 5, 36	Fridays: 76, 92
Tuesdays: 43, 57	Saturdays: 143, and a
Wednesdays: 64, 65	canticle from Deuteronomy

Prime. Four sections of Psalm 119 on Sundays;

on other days 3 Psalms each from Psalms 1, 2, 6-20.

Terce, Sext, and Nones. On Sundays, three sections of Psalm 119 for each service; on weekdays 3 Psalms each in course from Psalms 120-128.

Vespers. Four Psalms each day in course, except those otherwise appointed, from Psalms 110-118, 129-147.

Compline. Psalms 4, 91, and 134 daily.

By the late fourth century there is some evidence that morning and evening services of psalmody and prayer were available daily in cathedrals and larger city churches. *The Apostolic Constitutions*, a church order written at Antioch about 380, mentions them and notes that Psalm 63 was sung at the morning office and 143 in the evening.[99] John Cassian says that Psalm 51 was used in churches in Italy along with the customary Psalms 148-150 at Lauds, [100] and St. Benedict in his *Rule* refers to a service of Lauds at Rome.[101] These services were no doubt in charge of the secular (i.e., non-monastic) clergy. At Jerusalem the Bishop and other clergy took some part in the Daily Offices which the monks performed in the cathedral and churches of the city.[102]

In the Western churches the secular clergy became involved in, and finally required to observe the full round of Daily Offices developed by the monks. It is not possible to trace in detail the steps of this process.[103] At Rome the Offices were formulated during the fifth, sixth, and seventh centuries under the influence of the monasteries attached to the great basilicas. When Charlemagne imposed the Roman service books throughout his kingdom, the Roman Daily Offices were also required for all clergy assigned to cathedrals and parish churches. In the regulations *(capitularies)* of 802 it is stated:

> 2. That every priest assist at the daily prayers for the bishop by whom he is governed.
>
> 8. That all priests ring the bells of their churches at the proper hours of the day and night and pray the sacred offices to God at those times, and that they teach their people how God is to be adored, and at what hours.

The distribution of Psalms in the ancient Roman Offices is similar in pattern to that of the *Rule* of St. Benedict. The sequential course of psalmody in each week is largely divided, unless otherwise appointed, between Nocturns (Psalms 1-109) and Vespers (Psalms 110-147). Lauds has daily fixed Psalms— 51, 63, 67, 148-150—along with one daily variable, Psalms 100, 5, 43, 65, 90, 143, and 92. The "day hours" divide Psalm 119 throughout the week, with Psalms 118 on Sundays and 54 on weekdays. Compline has the three Psalms: 4, 91, and 134.

13. Dialogic Versicles and Responses

One of the characteristic features of the Daily Offices is the use of dialog between the officiant and the congregation. These short forms are generally called "versicles and responses," often abbreviated in service books with the letters V. and R. They are most commonly taken from the Psalms, and are employed as invocations, biddings, or petitions. Sometimes they are introductory; at other times they are transitional or complementary. It is possible that these forms were suggested by the more ancient biddings that punctuate the Eucharistic rite: "The Lord be with you, etc." [104] or "Let us give thanks, etc." [105] But the versicles and responses of the Daily Offices are much more varied and extensive in both content and intention.

Already in his *Rule* St. Benedict prescribed the opening versicles of the several Offices, probably following a well-established tradition. These are addresses to God for assistance and are invocational in character. Since Nocturns was the first Office of each day—beginning usually after midnight—its opening versicles served as an invocation for the whole daily round:

V. O Lord, open thou my lips,
R. And my mouth shall show forth thy praise.
[Psalms 51:15]

For the other Offices the following was prescribed:

V. O God, make speed to save us.
R. O Lord, make haste to help us.
[Psalm 70:1][106]

In St. Benedict's *Rule* there are references to other antiphons, responsories, and *preces* ("prayers") in the Daily Offices, which had become traditional, and which in the course of the Middle Ages were greatly elaborated in the Offices of both the monks and the secular clergy. The Psalms of the day were sung antiphonally in the manner of the antiphonal Psalms of the liturgy (see Section 8 above). Two choral groups of the community sang the verses of the Psalm alternately, with an antiphon sung before and after the Psalm, and also after each verse or group of verses. In the Daily Offices, these antiphons were more often selected from a verse of the appointed Psalm, and they varied with the seasons of the Church Year. After the lessons a responsory was sung, similar in form to the responsorial Gradual of the liturgy (see Section 7 above). The texts of these were sometimes taken from the Psalms, more often from other books of Scripture.[107]

At the conclusion of Nocturns on Sundays the canticle *Te Deum* was appointed after the final lesson and responsory. At a very early time this great hymn had attached to it a series of versicles; [108] all but one of them, the central petition, are derived from the Psalms:

V. O LORD, save your people, and bless your heritage;

R.   shepherd them, and bear them up for ever.   [28:10]

V. Day by day we will bless you,

R.   and praise your Name for ever and ever.
                                              [145:2]

V. Lord, keep us this day without sin;

R.   have mercy on us, Lord, have mercy on us.   [123:3]

V. Lord, let your loving-kindness be upon us,

R.   even as we put our trust in you. [33:22]

V. In you, Lord, I take refuge;

        let me never be put to shame.   [31:1]

At Lauds and Vespers, following the lesson and responsory, a Gospel canticle was sung—the *Benedictus* and the *Magnificat*, respectively. These were followed by *preces*, which generally followed this pattern:

Kyrie eleison, etc.

The Lord's Prayer

V. I said, Lord, be merciful to me;

R.   heal my soul, for I have sinned against you.   [41:4]

V. How long, O Lord, before you return,

R.   and have pity on your servants. [90:13]

V. Lord, let your loving-kindness be upon us,

R.   even as we put our trust in you. [33:22]

V. Let your priests be clothed with righteousness,

R.   and let your saints shout for joy. [132:9]

V. O Lord, give victory to the King,

R.   and hear us when we call to you. [20:9]

V. Lord, save your people, and bless your heritage;

R.   shepherd them, and bear them up for
         ever.   [28:10]

V. Remember your congregation,

R.   which you have purchased of old [74:2]

V. Peace be within your walls,
         and prosperity within your palaces.
                                          [122:7]

There were, of course, many variations in these versicles from church to church and monastery to monastery. But one will recognize here the origin of the *preces* at the morning and evening Offices of both the Lutheran service books and the Anglican Book of Common Prayer.[109]

Similar versicles concluded the "day hours" of Prime, Terce, Sext, and Nones. At Compline, the versicles from the Psalms form the responsory after the lesson from Jeremiah 14:9, and precede the Gospel canticle *Nunc Dimittis:*

V. Into your hands, Lord, I commend my spirit.

R. Into your hands, Lord, I commend my spirit.

V. For you have redeemed us, O Lord, God of truth.

R. I commend my spirit. [31:5]

V. Glory be to the Father, and to the Son, and
     to the Holy Spirit.
R. Into your hands, Lord, I commend my spirit.
V. Keep us as the apple of your eye;
R. Hide us under the shadow of your wings.
                                                    [17:8]

Many other versicles are scattered through the Latin
Offices. Among those frequently used in services today are:

V. Our help is in the Name of the Lord,
R.   who made heaven and earth.   [124:8]
V. Lord, hear our prayer,
R.   and let our cry come unto you. [102:1]

14. Select Psalms for Special Devotion

The liturgical Offices were not the sum of the monk's devotion. The days were filled with private prayer and psalmody. In the early days of Egyptian monasticism, it was not uncommon for monks to recite the entire Psalter once a day; and this custom became a common feature of ascetical discipline among the early Celtic monks of Ireland, whose stringent practices carried on the traditions of the desert solitaries of Egypt. St. Benedict's *Rule*, however, was noted for its moderation, the result of his own unsatisfactory experience with excessive mortification. In the twenty-four hour day approximately eight hours were devoted to worship, eight to work, and eight to rest.

In the West, from the ninth century, monastic regulations began to increase the requirements of devotional practices over and beyond the daily round of Offices. The employment of lay brothers to do the major manual work left the monks with more time for worship. In the great monastery of Cluny, founded in 910, and its daughter houses the round of worship engaged most of the monks' waking hours. Many of these new devotions were taken up also in the Breviaries of the secular clergy. We shall mention only several of them that involved a larger use of the Psalms.[110]

The *Trina oratio* was a threefold devotion before Matins, before Prime in summer or Terce in winter, and after Compline. It consisted of a visit to the altars of the monastery church, followed by recital of groups of Psalms for various intentions: for the monks and the faithful living, for the king and queen, and for the faithful departed. In some places these were the fifteen "Gradual Psalms," i.e. the Songs of Ascents, Psalms 120-134 (see Section 3 above). In others, they were the seven Penitential Psalms: 6, 32, 38, 51, 102, 130, 143. Both of these groups came to be a substantial part of daily devotion before or after one of the day hours. Another group of Psalms known as *psalmi familiares* were recited for benefactors and friends—two, three, or four, after each of the hours. The choice varied from place to place, but generally included Psalms 51, 57, 70, and 142.

An Office for the Dead began to be observed daily from the ninth century, and developed into three Offices of Vespers, Nocturns and Lauds, recited in addition to the regular course. In the Roman Breviary the Psalms appointed are:

Vespers: 116, 120, 121, 130, 138
Nocturns: 5-7, 23-25, 40-42
Lauds: 51, 65, 63, 67, 148-150.

From the eleventh century there spread the little

Office of Our Lady—a complete but shorter round of canonical hours. The Psalms were generally those proper to the regular Offices, except for Nocturns which had proper Psalms: 8, 19, 24, or sometimes 45 or 87.

The importance of these devotions added to an already lengthy schedule of daily worship in that in the later Middle Ages these were included in devotional books for the laity, whether in Latin or the vernacular. Known as the Book of Hours or (in England) the Primer, these books included the Creed, Lord's Prayer, the Ten Commandments, and the Gradual and Penitential Psalms, the Office of the Dead, and the Little Office of Our Lady, plus other sundry devotions. Granted that not all of the laity could read, or much less afford books, these handbooks of lay devotion provided some of the basics of praise and prayer related to the liturgy of the church. They form part of the background of the Reformation adaptations of the Daily Offices in the vernacular.

15. The Reform of the Daily Offices

In the course of the Middle Ages the Daily Offices tended to take on more and more elaboration, and not only by the additional devotions described above (Section 14). On the major saints' days the Offices were doubled—those for the day and those with proper formularies for the saints. It was too much for most priests to bear. In the thirteenth century a radical shortening was made, first in the Offices of the Roman Curia, and then in the Breviaries of the itinerant Franciscan friars. The double office was eliminated, and the office of the saints was substituted, on the proper days, for the regular office of the day. Lessons were shortened to a few verses. Yet the number of the saints' days increased, with frequent use of "common propers." The result was that the ancient regular course of psalmody was seriously impaired by the constant substitution of fixed proper Psalms for the commemoration of the saints.

By the sixteenth century there were many cries for reform within the Roman Catholic Church itself, well before the outbreak of the Reformation. Pope Clement VII (1523-1534) charged a learned Spanish

Cardinal, Francisco Quignonez, to prepare a revision of the Breviary. This appeared in 1535 (second edition, 1536), and despite immediate objections it became very popular.[111] In forty years it went through one hundred editions! First of all, Quinonez gave up the idea of choral recitation in favor of private use. Antiphons, responsories, versicles, and hymns were eliminated; and though the entire Psalter was appointed to be read once a week, no Psalm was repeated, and for each office three Psalms were assigned. These were to be read without interruption by proper Psalms for a feast.

So radical a revision was not likely to find favor in official circles. The Council of Trent, which opened in 1545, gave some attention to the problem, but the disagreements as to the shape of the reformed Breviary led the Council Fathers to place the matter in the hands of the Pope. In 1568 Pope Pius V issued a new Breviary, substantially similar to the ancient Roman one. The weekly distribution of the Psalter was protected from over-much interruption from privileged saints' days. The accessory devotions were no longer obligatory, and even the long weekday *preces* were limited to Advent and Lent and a few other occasions.[112]

Luther was prepared to continue the tradition of the Daily Offices in his Latin Mass of 1523, except for the observance of the saints' days. He valued the daily reading of the Psalms and lessons. But he felt that Matins (Lauds) and Vespers were sufficient, each with three Psalms, and with the Scriptural responsories after the lessons. In the German Mass of 1526, he reiterated his preferences for the two Offices, but unfortunately he did not go all the way in a vernacular service. He wanted to keep the chanting of the Psalms in Latin so that the youth in the schools would continue to know and use this language. Thus the Church Orders provided the Latin Psalter, often with the old plainsong psalm-tones, assigning Psalms 1-109 to Matins and Psalms 110-150 to Vespers. Hence as Luther Reed has said,

> The great development of vernacular hymnody, . . . the dissolution of monastic communities, and the discontinuance of corporate clerical worship, eventually caused the chanting of the psalms and the use of the traditional psalm tones to disappear almost entirely from Lutheran worship.[113]

In the Church of England, the reform of the Offices made by Archbishop Cranmer became by contrast a lasting and successful achievement. Inspired by both Quignonez and Luther, Cranmer reduced and simplified the sevenfold Offices into two: Morn- and Evening Prayer. As in Quinonez' Breviary, all antiphons, responsories, hymns, and most versicles were eliminated. The Psalter was distributed in course reading over a month, rather than a week, with approximately three or four Psalms for each service, depending upon their length.[114] In the Second Prayer Book of 1552, Psalms 100, 98, and 67, were provided as alternatives to the Gospel canticles, in response to "Puritan" objections that regarded these canticles as lessons rather than as hymns. As finally shaped,

through the Prayer Books of 1549 and 1552, the
Offices were ordered as follows:

Morning Prayer
   Scriptural Sentences and Penitential Order
      (1552)
   Lord's Prayer
   Versicles (Psalms 51:15, 70:1) and *Gloria Patri*
   Venite, Psalm 95
   Psalms (as appointed)
   Old Testament Lesson
   Te Deum or *Benedicite*
   New Testament Lesson
   Benedictus or Psalm 100 (1552)
   Creed (1552), Kyries, Lord's Prayer, and
      Suffrages
   Collect of the Day and two other fixed Collects

Evening Prayer
   Scriptural Sentences and Penitential Order
      (1552)
   Lord's Prayer
   Versicles (Psalm 70:1) and *Gloria Patri*
   Psalms (as appointed)
   Old Testament Lesson
   Magnificat or Psalm 98 (1552)
   New Testament Lesson
   Nunc Dimittis or Psalm 67 (1552)
   Creed (1552), Kyries, Lord's Prayer, and
      Suffrages
   Collect of the Day and two other fixed Collects

The Anglican Daily Offices were designed for the
laity as well as the clergy, so that both would be

edified by the reading and meditation upon the Scriptures. Hence there was a loss in the variables of antiphons, responsories, and such other changes according to the Church Year, which gave liveliness to the routine of the old Latin Offices, and in a substantial way to the recovered Lutheran Offices of modern times. Such variables, however, are confusing to the laity, who do not have the professional training in liturgics afforded to the clergy. There is a monotony of structure in the Anglican Offices, but their very simplicity and regularity have made them much beloved by the laity—so much so, that in many Anglican churches the Daily Offices became the preferred form of public worship on most Sundays of the year.

On the other hand, it should be said that the recovery of Matins and Vespers in the Lutheran tradition, since the late nineteenth century, has owed a great deal to the Anglican experience of the Offices, at least among Lutherans in English speaking countries. In the structures of the two Offices, and especially in the provision for two lessons from the Old and the New Testament, respectively, the morning and evening services of Lutherans and Anglicans exhibit a close similarity.[115]

IV.

Renewal of
Psalmody Today

16. The Revival of Psalmody in the Liturgy

The recovery of psalmody in the Eucharistic liturgy has been one of the notable achievements of the reforms in recent times of the usages of the churches of the Reformation. In the Lutheran churches this began with the revival of their historic orders of service in the latter part of nineteenth century. In the United States the pre-Reformation series of Introits was restored in the *Common Service* of 1888 and the Graduals in the *Common Service Book* of 1917. These have been retained in more recent Lutheran service books and hymnals. They are, however, the truncated psalmody of the old Latin rite, consisting of one or two psalm verses with their antiphons or refrains.

The current series of *Contemporary Worship,* prepared for provisional use by the Inter-Lutheran Commission on Worship, has suggested a new approach which is similar to recent reforms in the Roman Catholic Church. In place of the traditional Introits, an "Entrance Hymn" is appointed, although in places where Psalms are preferred, in whole or in part, these would undoubtedly be permissible as a substitute for or addition to the hymn. The Gradual Psalm, however, has been restored to a full Psalm or at least a larger portion of one than that provided in the ancient series. The selections are listed, with refrains, in No. 6 on The Church Year, Calendar and Lectionary. Rubrical notations of their place after the first lesson have been included in Nos. 2, 3, and 7 for the Holy Communion, Marriage Service and Holy Baptism, respectively. As in the revised Roman rite, the Gradual is considered "a major part of the service, not merely convenient transition pieces" (No. 6, p. 28).

In the Anglican churches restoration of the medieval psalmody began unofficially in the later nineteenth century in many "Anglo-Catholic" parishes influenced by the Catholic revival known as the Oxford Movement. Much interest was also shown in adapting the medieval plainsong to English texts, as in the publications of the Plainsong and Mediaeval Music Society, founded in 1888. *The English Hymnal* of 1906 (also unofficial) contained the texts of the psalm-propers to be used in the Holy Communion at the traditional places.

As we have seen, the permission to sing a metrical psalm before and after any service, authorized by Queen Elizabeth I (see Section 10 above), continued to be followed in Anglican services; but by the nineteenth century hymns had largely supplanted the use of metrical versions of the Psalms. This custom was officially authorized in the American revision of The Book of Common Prayer completed in 1892, which included, in addition to hymns, "Anthems in the words of Holy Scripture or of the Book of Common Prayer." Such anthems would obviously include, where desired, texts from the Psalter. In the revision completed in 1928, the American church also restored the use of hymns or anthems after the Epistle and during the Offertory and the Communion.

Several Anglican revisions of the Prayer Book in the past two decades have given permission for similar hymns, anthems, or Psalms at the Introit, Gradual, Offertory, and Communion. The Canadian Prayer Book of 1959 provides a table of Psalms for optional use at the Eucharist for the Introit and Gradual; and the Supplement to the Book of Common Prayer for India prints in full proper Introit Psalms for Sundays and major Holy Days.[116] A proposed revision of the Church Year prepared by the Church of England Liturgical Commission suggests two Psalms selections for its two-year cycle of lessons for the Holy Communion.[117] These are based only in general on the traditional assignments. The Episcopal Church in the United States, in its present process of revision of the Prayer Book, has noted for optional use two selections from the Psalter (averaging six to eight verses) for the Holy Eucharist.[118] At present the Standing Liturgical Commission has prepared for consideration a schedule similar to that of the Lutheran one in *Contemporary Worship* No. 6.

The Reformed or Presbyterian churches have always used the metrical versions of the Psalms, though in modern times other hymns have tended more and more to supplant them. These churches have not observed the Christian Year until recently; hence they do not have a fixed schedule of Psalms. In the Church of Scotland a growing interest in liturgical worship has been fostered by the Church Service Society, founded in 1860. Since 1923, official service books have provided psalmody at the traditional places, whether metrical or non-metrical; and this is continued in the latest edition of *The Book of Common Order* of 1940. In the United States, the third edition of *The Book of Common Worship* (1946) refers only to hymns, although a lectionary at the end of the book lists proper Psalms for the Sunday services. *The Worshipbook* of 1970, containing services and hymns, has a section on "The Christian Year" that suggests "Responsive Readings" taken chiefly from the Psalms for use with seasonal lessons.[119]

The new Mass rite of the Roman Catholic Church, consequent to the reforms authorized by the Second Vatican Council, allows a continued use of the ancient psalm-propers contained in the *Graduale* of Pope Pius X, promulgated in 1908. A larger flexibility is now allowed in Pope Paul's VI's official *Missale Romanum* of 1970. Antiphons for the Introit and Communion are provided if there is no other song. But in place of the older Introits, Offertories, and Communions, a hymn or song is allowed, subject to approval by the several conferences of Bishops. These songs, which may include Psalms, are sung alternately by the choir and people, by the cantor and people, or entirely by the people or the choir alone. The Gradual, however, is "an integral part of the liturgy of the Word," and is taken from the lectionary. It is sung by a cantor with responses by the people. The texts of the Gradual are much longer than those in the older rite. Provision is also made for seasonal Graduals to help the congregation in learning to sing refrains.

Thus in the liturgical churches today the Psalms come back into their own, but not in restrictive texts or ways of rendition. Whether sung or said, they may be rendered in unison by the choir or the people, or in responsive methods in various combinations of cantors, choirs, people, or alternate groupings of choirs and people (see Section 19 below, for various musical settings).

17. Psalms for the Christian Year

Since the Reformation era, the Roman Catholic, Lutheran, and Anglican churches have maintained in common the ordering of the Christian Year as it was finally developed in the western church by the end of the sixth century. The principal difference has been in the naming of the Sundays after the feast of Pentecost. In the early tenth century there was instituted in Liège a special feast in honor of the Holy Trinity on the Octave or First Sunday after Pentecost. This feast became popular in the churches of northern Europe, including England, and gradually the Sundays following were named "after Trinity" instead of "after Pentecost." The Roman church kept the older naming, and did not officially adopt the feast of the Holy Trinity until 1334.

Similarly, the three churches continued the schedule of Epistles and Gospels for the Sundays that derive from the old Roman lectionaries fixed in the sixth-seventh centuries. There are some discrepancies, however, since the modern Roman Missal made certain alterations in the medieval lists.[120] The Lutherans and Anglicans kept the older schedules, with a few minor changes. In his *Formula Missae* (Latin Mass) of 1523, Luther expressed some dissatisfaction with the accustomed use, especially with the Epistles, since they seemed to give too much emphasis to "works." But he was not prepared to attempt any revision, "as nothing ungodly is read," for he considered that vernacular preaching would make up for any lack.

The Second Vatican Council, in its *Constitution on the Sacred Liturgy* completed in 1963, called for an overall review of both the seasons of the Christian Year and the lessons of the Eucharist:

> Chapter II, Section 51: The treasures of the Bible are to be opened up more lavishly, so that richer fare may be provided for the faithful at the table of God's Word. In this way a more representative portion of the holy Scriptures will be read to the people over a set cycle of years.

> Chapter V, Sections 107-108: The liturgical year is to be revised so that the traditional customs and discipline of the sacred seasons can be preserved or restored to meet the conditions of modern times. . . . The minds of the faithful must be directed primarily toward the feasts of the Lord in which the mysteries of salvation are celebrated in the course of the year. Therefore, the Proper of Time shall be given the preference which is its due over the feasts of the saints, so that the entire cycle of the

mysteries of salvation can be suitably recalled.[121]

The Consilium for Implementing the Constitu-
tion completed these tasks with the papal promul-
gation of a new Calendar and a new Order of Les-
sons for the Mass in 1969.[122] Notable changes in the
Church Year were the suppression of the three Pre-
Lenten Sundays, the institution of a feast of the
Baptism of Our Lord on the First Sunday after the
Epiphany, the title of "Sunday of the Passion" given
to Palm Sunday, and the inclusion of the feast of
Pentecost within the great fifty days of Easter.

As for the Eucharistic lectionary, it was now devised on a three year cycle, with the addition of an
Old Testament reading to the Epistles and Gospels.
In this new ordering most of the New Testament is
read in the course of the three years, while the Old
Testament selections are made chiefly to provide
background to the Gospel lections. On the Sundays
and major Holy Days of the chief seasons, the lessons are "proper" to the day or season; but on the
"green" Sundays after the Epiphany and after Pentecost, the Epistles follow a schedule of sequential
readings not used in the other seasons. Of the Gospels Matthew is read in Year A, Mark in Year B,
and Luke in Year C. Readings from the Gospel of
John, not used otherwise, are inserted within the
Markan lections, since the latter Gospel is of shorter
length.

The excellence of the new schedules has led to
their adoption with some changes in the revised
Eucharistic rites of the Lutheran, Episcopalian, and

Presbyterian churches in America.[123] In some cases the Roman lections are lengthened. More variation is made in the Roman Old Testament lections—in part because the new Lutheran and Presbyterian services do not employ lessons from the Old Testament Apocrypha. Also the major changes in the Christian Year have been adopted, through unofficial consultation, by the three Protestant Churches.

The new Roman Lectionary includes Gradual Psalms—now much lengthened—to follow the Old Testament lesson throughout the three year cycle. The Alleluia chant has also been revised and is placed after the Epistle. This is a restoration of the ancient pattern. The traditional assignment of certain Psalms to the principal seasons and holy days is still preserved. So far, only the Lutherans have adopted the same basic schedule of Graduals (see Section 16 above); but the Episcopalians are considering a similar listing for their current revision of the Prayer Book. The Lutheran directives are quite correct in noting that the Gradual Psalms are a "corporate utterance" and not "additional lessons." [124] They are, nonetheless, in the sequence of lessons a renewal of "David's prophecy" (see Section 6 above).

18. New Translations

Vernacular translations of the Bible, in whole or in part, have never ceased since the Reformation period. Especially in our own century has this endeavor been constant and popular. This circumstance derives from advances of scholarship in our knowledge of biblical languages and customs, their cognate cultural backgrounds in the Near Eastern world, and also more ancient manuscripts than those known in previous generations.[125]

Yet few of these modern translations have influenced the texts read and sung in the liturgical services of English congregations until very recent times. They have remained as aids to study by preachers, devout lay people, and students in Bible classes. In public worship, the Authorized (King James) Version of 1611 has remained dominant, except for the older Coverdale version of the Psalter and certain other Scriptural passages used in the Prayer Books of the Anglican Churches. Only in the last two decades have many pastors and priests adopted the reading of lessons from contemporary translations.

In 1945 Pope Pius XII issued a new Latin translation of the Psalter based upon the ancient Hebrew text, for use in the Daily Offices of the Breviary for clergy and monastic communities, to replace the older "Vulgate" Psalter. As always, a new translation of an old and familiar text brought both approval and dismay. Yet it produced a spate of English translations designed for a better comprehension of the Psalter not only by the clergy and religious, but by the lay people also.[126] It is the Hebrew text underlying Pope Pius' Psalter that forms the basis of the two officially approved translations for English-speaking Roman Catholics: *The Jerusalem Bible* of 1966 and *The New American Bible* of 1970. Another approved text is the Grail version of the Psalms, which is designed for singing to the melodic patterns of Father Joseph Gelineau, S.J. (see Section 19 below).[127]

Official liturgies of the Lutheran churches using English in their worship have until recently depended upon the King James Version of 1611, e.g., the Introits and Graduals, and the selection of 114 Psalms, printed in the 1958 *Service Book and Hymnal.* In the current series of proposed services known as *Contemporary Worship,* prepared by the Inter-Lutheran Commission on Worship, greater freedom is employed in the translation of Psalter texts. No. 6 on the Church Year, however, gives references to the Propers from the Revised Standard Version, though other recent translations are noted and accepted. A notable modern translation of the Psalter by a Lutheran scholar, designed for both public and private use, is that of Richard S. Hanson.[128]

The version of the Psalter in the Anglican Prayer Books has remained with slight modifications that of Miles Coverdale (see Sections 10 and 15 above). For many years this version has been the subject of criticism. Both individual scholars and official church commissions have suggested revisions that modernize the language and conform the translation more closely to the original Hebrew text. Many of these proposals began to bear fruit in the Anglican revisions of the Prayer Book in the 1920s. Today, two official revisions of the Prayer Book Psalter are in experimental use—one in the Church of England, the other in the Episcopal Church in the United States.[129] The latter is more contemporary in its style and language.

Two other recent translations have received favorable attention. One has been prepared by the American Bible Society, *The Psalms for Modern Man* (1970)—part of its larger project of "Today's English Version."[130] The translation is in free, rhythmic verse; and, as the preface states, it "seeks to express the meaning of the Hebrew text in words and forms accepted as standard by people everywhere who employ English as a means of communication." The other is a selection of fifty Psalms, by a group of Dutch scholars, made available in an effective English translation in 1968.[131] This work avoids a word-for word translation, and employs a variety of verse and strophic forms. It is much enhanced by notes that explain both the Old Testament context and the New Testament fulfillment of the Psalms.

19. Singing the Psalms

The singing of the Psalms today in the Church's worship continues the various ancient patterns. Modern settings provide great flexibility in adapting them to the resources of congregations and choirs. There is, of course, a rich repertoire of Psalm texts composed for choirs of mixed voices comparable to anthems which only a trained choir can perform. These do not concern us here, although there is no reason to exclude such settings in places with choirs adequate to render them at appropriate places in the liturgy. In fact, as we have seen (Sections 7-8 above), the use of psalmody at the Eucharist was originally a function of the choir in accompanying the basic processions of the liturgy—the Introits, Graduals, Offertories, and Communions.[132]

What is notable about the current renaissance of psalmody in the Eucharist is the interest in congregational involvement in singing them. In small churches, where there may be only a few singers to lead, it is necessary for the congregation to be involved if there is to be any psalmody at all. When the Daily Offices of Matins and Vespers are observed, it is all the more necessary, because of the nature of these Offices, that the congregation have a part in the Psalms in unison or harmonic settings that are within the range of its abilities.

The oldest and most widespread method of singing the Psalms is the chant: simple melodic formulae of medium pitch and tonal range [133] which are repeated for each verse of a Psalm. Chants may be sung in unison or in harmonized versions. Instrumental accompaniment is not necessary; its use is largely a matter of taste. When used it should be designed solely to support the singers and control the pitch. It should never "lead" the voices. This brings us to the most important thing about chanting: namely, rhythm. We have seen (Section 1 above) that the Psalm texts are not metrical; the rhythm is created by the pulse or "tone" of the principal syllables. Hence the rhythm of chanting is the same as that of natural speech. In a very real sense, chanting is but a heightened form of speech. This principle applies to both unison and harmonized chants; and this is why any accompaniments must not force, drag, or in any way interfere with the rhythm of the words. [134]

Chant forms of psalmody are perfectly suited to the structure of Hebrew poetry. Each verse or line of a Psalm contains a complete thought; hence each melodic line is designed for a single verse. There is no carry over of words or of melody from verse to verse. Each verse, according to the principle of "parallelism of verse members" (see Section 1 above), has normally two parts (stichs), sometimes three and occasionally four. Chant melodies always have two parts: 1) reciting note and mediation; 2) reciting note and cadence. In unison chants the first half may begin with an intonation,[135] but this is not customary in harmonized chants. Where the Psalm verse has an uneven number of stichs, that is three, the first two or the last two are assigned to the first or second half of the melodic line, depending upon the length and sense of the extra stich. For example, in Psalm 19:5-6, the melodic arrangement of the stichs would be as follows:

First part:

5. In the depths of the sea he pitched a tent for the sun,

Second part:

who comes out from his canopy as a bridegroom,
and rejoices as a champion in a race.

First part:

6. He rises from one edge of the heavens,
and makes his circuit to the other;

Second part:

and nothing is hidden from his heat.

Short Psalms may be sung directly throughout by the whole body of singers. But in longer Psalms this is tedious, and attention is increased by dividing into antiphonal groups, which alternate from one to the other verse by verse. There is no justification for alternating by half verses.[136] In certain Psalms that have an obvious strophic structure the antiphonal singing may be by strophes. Where these strophes have refrains, it may be effective for the whole group to join in the refrains (for examples, see Section 1 above). Another effective way of antiphonal singing is to alternate verses between choir and congregation. In such cases, the choir may sing harmonized versions of the melody, or perhaps even polyphonic settings.[137]

The ancient methods of antiphonal and responsorial psalmody also provide variant ways of giving life and interest to psalm-singing. The simpler form is responsorial. A cantor or cantors sing the verses of the Psalm, and the choir and congregation respond after each verse or group of verses with a fixed refrain, either in unison or in harmony. Psalms with "Hallelujah" lend themselves readily to this form. Antiphonal psalmody, i.e., Psalms with an antiphon, is a bit more complex, but provides more variations in rendition. The following methods are feasible:

	1.	2.
Antiphon	Cantor	Cantor
Psalm verse(s)	Congregation	Choir
Antiphon	Choir	Congregation
Psalm verse(s)	Congregation	Choir
Gloria Patri	All	Congregation
Antiphon	Choir	Cantor and Choir

Other combinations are possible. Normally, a cantor must sing the antiphon first to give its melody; when it is repeated, either the choir or the congregation or both may sing it. Similarly the Psalm verses may be divided among the cantors, choir, and congregation. To render the Psalms in this way, however, the congregation must have in its hands both the texts and the music. Even for responsorial psalmody, the congregation should have text and music of its refrains, unless these are simple enough and often repeated so that they know them by heart.

Plainsong

Plainsong, often called Gregorian chant, is the classic unisonal music of the western church.[138] Its origins are obscure, as are its relationships with other ancient chants such as the Byzantine and the Ambrosian (Church of Milan).[139] Commonly associated with the name of Pope Gregory the Great (590-604), the chant cannot be considered as his composition, though he was probably the first to make a definitive arrangement of it for the Roman rite. The oldest manuscripts of the texts of the chants are not earlier than the mid-eighth century, and the earliest manuscripts providing some kind of identifiable melodies hardly reach back earlier than about A.D. 900. It is the glory of the Benedictine monks of Solemnes Abbey, France, in the nineteenth century to have recovered through careful study of the manuscripts an authentic musical transcription, along with learned studies of tonality, rhythm, and nuances of rendition. Their work was officially approved in the Roman *Graduale* for the Mass (1907) and *Antiphonale* for the Daily Offices (1912) by Pope Pius X. These are the mines from which all modern versions of plainsong and adaptations of them are drawn.

For a half century Roman Catholic choirmasters

struggled to train choirs, often with conspicuous success, in mastering this treasure of liturgical song. It was idealized as the perfect marriage of liturgical text and music—a supernatural gift, as it were, to the church. So the French novelist J. K. Huysmans regarded it:

> "Ah! the true creator of plain music, the unknown author who cast into the brain of man the seed of plain chant, was the Holy Ghost." [140]

Today, with the revolutionary changes in Roman Catholic worship, brought about by the Second Vatican Council's reforms and the introduction of the vernacular, Roman Catholic musicians are having second thoughts. The Abbot Primate of the Benedictine Order, Dom Rembert Weakland, has written:

> This aesthetic of church music justified music as art in church by describing it as a gift to glorify God—the sublimest creative act of man being given back to God. It was like a package wrapped in a golden cloth with a golden ribbon. Whether the people understood the contents of the gift was secondary. The more aesthetically satisfying the gift, the more pleasing to God. . . .

> We cannot preserve the treasures of the past without coming to terms with false liturgical orientations that gave birth to this music; nor can we preserve them according to the false aesthetic judgments of the last century. They can only be preserved for that

which they are: beautiful pieces of music that served the past generations of the Church and of which we are rightfully proud. . . .

On the other hand, if the liturgical experience is to be primarily the communal sensitivity that I am one with my brother next to me and that our song is our common twentieth-century response to God's word here and now coming to us in our twentieth-century situation, it will be something quite different. We will not expect to find the holy in music by archaicism, but in our own twentieth-century idiom. We will seek to share our common experience without looking for a false kind of objectivism, a false aesthetic that simulates union with God because it seems superhuman. There is no supernatural music—not of the past, nor of the present, nor of the future.[141]

This is the plea of a learned and sensitive churchman and musician. Yet it probably reflects a judgment based upon centuries of liturgical use of a Latin rite in which the people had little active part. It also accords with the view of many Roman Catholic musicians that plainsong is only suitable for Latin texts which are sung by a trained choir. It ignores the long experience of Lutherans and Anglicans with plainsong melodies and psalm-tones adapted to the vernacular, whether for the Eucharist or the Daily Offices. Hence Roman Catholic composers of music for the liturgy, though inspired by the free melodic rhythms of plainsong, tend to devise new melodies and harmonizations in a modern idiom, be it designed for choirs or for congregations.

There is no doubt that plainsong, except for a few popular hymn tunes, is difficult for many congregations, especially if one seeks the niceties of performance according to the Solesmes tradition. The modal tonality is strange, and the lack of accentual rhythm is foreign to the music with which they are most familiar. Yet it is the experience of many Lutheran and Anglican churches that congregations are able to sing plainsong with gusto and enthusiasm, if not always with artistic results. The principal musical problem is the final note of the cadence of the melodies. In Latin texts the final note is always rendered lightly, since in Latin there are no final syllables that are accented. In English, however, a final syllable may often be a strong one (masculine ending) rather than an unaccented one (feminine ending). For example:

Psalm 95 (the *Venite*)
  1 Come, let us sing to the *Lord;*
      let us shout for joy to the Rock of our
      sal*va*tion

  2 Let us come before his presence with
        thanks*giv*ing,
      and raise a loud shout to him in *psalms.*

In mediations and endings there is often a tendency to come down rather heavily on "Lord" and "psalms" (masculine endings), but also on "-tion" and "-ing" (feminine endings). The same is true of monosyllabic words at the end, such as "you," "me," "him."

Harmonized Chants

The harmonized, or Anglican, chant is seldom if ever used by Roman Catholics, but has been widely used by Lutherans and Anglicans. Its roots go back to the English Reformation, when composers for the Prayer Book rites, such as Thomas Tallis, provided harmonies of soprano, alto, and bass voices about the chant melodies sung in the tenor. The rhythm was exactly like plainsong, except that in the cadences there was often some trace of polyphony. Many were modal in tonality. During the period of Cromwell's Commonwealth, however, when the Prayer Book rites were proscribed, much of this tradition, along with a great wealth of polyphonic settings of service music and anthems, was lost. At the Restoration of the monarchy under Charles II in 1660 a new taste for church music was introduced—music in strict time according to the modalities of major and minor scales. "Anglican chants" in the new style began to proliferate. Melodies, more like little hymn tunes, were placed in the soprano voice, and even bar lines were introduced to measure the mediations and cadences.

Anglican psalmody, as we have seen (Section 15 above) was largely confined to the Daily Offices. In the nineteenth century many cathedrals and larger parish churches with professional choirs published their own Psalters, replete with their own pointings of texts for chanting and supplied with many extravagant "tunes" in range of melody and chromatic harmonization. In recent times, both in England and America, there has been a reaction in order to restore the free rather than the metrical rhythm in singing chants, and a greater sensitivity to those chants that are suitable for congregations as well as choirs.

Two schools of thought have arisen about the pointing of texts for Anglican chant. One position, led by the late Canon Charles Winfred Douglas, the chief editor of *The American Psalter* (1930), has insisted upon a pointing similar to plainsong, as harmonized by the Reformation English composers. In this system, the pointing is so devised that the last note of the mediation and of the final cadence has only one syllable. The other view, developed by the English Church's Royal College of Church Music, proposes what is called "speech rhythm." The chant is simply a vehicle for natural rhythms of speech, without any regard to metric measures and allowing two or even three syllables to be sung to notes of the mediation and cadence. Both schools, however, insist upon a free flow of the chant according to the sense of the words. Examples of the two methods may be thus illustrated:

Psalm 65

American Psalter

Thou O God art prais-ed in | Si - | on;
  and unto thee shall the vow be perform-ed
  | in Je- | ru-sa- | lem.

The Oxford Psalter

Thou O God art | prais'd in | Sion:
    and unto thee shall the | vow be per- |
    form'd in Je- | rusalem.

The secret of good harmonized chanting will always be the same as in unisonal chanting. The
rhythm of the words is primary. But in Anglican
chant, the melodic lines no less than the accompaniment must be subservient to this rhythm and never
control it. Any system of pointing will work provided this principle is maintained.[142]

Gelineau Psalmody

In recent times a new method of popular psalmody
has been created by Father Joseph Gelineau, a
French Jesuit. It was first introduced in connection with his translation of the Psalms for *La Sainte
Bible,* the original Jerusalem Bible, so named
since its direction was under the scholars of the
Dominicans' L'École Biblique in Jerusalem. It was
soon adapted to an English version by The Grail in
England, and has had a rapid spread and use in
English-speaking churches. The translations are in
free verse, set to melodies with a regular beat or
pulse, four to the measure. Each measure may have
one, two, three, or four syllables, with stress on the
first syllable of each measure, these being the important words of the line. Each Psalm also has one
or more antiphons, also metric and frequently repeated among the verses by the congregation with
the choir.

Father Gelineau's settings, with accompaniment, have inspired many imitators of his model. For some time it seemed that this new method, engaging congregations and choir (or cantors) in a joint rendering of the Psalms, might sweep the field. Some of the compositions have won a lasting place in the repertoire of liturgical song. But frequent repetition has tended to dull the original enthusiasm. This may be due either to the character of the melodies, or, more likely, to the monotony of the rhythms with their inevitable, regular beats. The Gelineau psalmody remains, no less, a significant ingredient in the current search of composers for an effective liturgical use of the Psalter.

Mixed Types

The situation today, especially in Lutheran and Roman Catholic churches where psalmody is an essential part of the liturgy, is a very mixed and eclectic one in musical settings. Unison and harmonized, metrical and non-metrical forms are used in varying combinations. But the rhythms are more flexible, the melodies more inventive, the harmonies more sparse or discordant. Instruments and voice are in more dialog (perhaps as in ancient psalmody in the Temple). There is considerable experiment in the deployment of cantors, choir, and congregation. Sometimes the people sing the antiphons or refrains, in other cases cantors or choir. The range of difficulty is wide—perhaps composers have always had in mind the abilities of their own choirs. There is no common pattern. Possibly this reflects the state of experimental liturgies themselves, or perhaps the pluralism that is a mark of contemporary Christianity in its ecumenical thrusts. What is encouraging is that the several church traditions use and borrow more from one another, and this includes the texts of biblical translations. There is a new ferment of creativity in the air—for the Psalms are again being recovered as the vehicles of Christian prayer and praise. (The bibliography, Section B, will include listings of some current resources with brief comments.)

20. Special Occasions:
Baptism, Marriage, and Burial

In the ancient church Psalms 23 and 42 are especially associated with Baptism; and these Psalms inspired the mosaics or fresco paintings in many baptisteries. The old Latin Missal of the Roman church preserved a relic of this usage in the appointment of Psalm 42:1-3 as a Tract at the Vigil of Easter, before the procession to the baptismal Font. At the Reformation, however, neither Luther nor the English Reformers included a Psalm in their revised baptismal rites.[143]

The new services of Baptism provide many choices from the Psalter, appointed after an Old Testament Lesson, at a baptismal Eucharist. Though the Psalm is specifically a Gradual, it may be rendered in any way suitable to the occasion and the presence of cantors, choir, and congregation:

Roman Catholic
  Infants: 23; 27 and 34 (selected verses).
  Adults (normally at the Easter Vigil): 23,
    126; and 8, 27, 32, 34, 42-43, 51, 63, 66, 89,
    (selected verses).

Lutheran: Contemporary Worship No. 7 (p. 17)
8, 23, 29, 34:1-9, 42:1-2a—43:3-4, 84, 93, 122.

Episcopal: Authorized Services 1973 (p. 14)
15, 23, 27, 42, 84, 87, 100, 122.

For many centuries the only church service for a married couple was the Nuptial Eucharist and Blessing, since the marriage contract and vows were taken before lay magistrates. Not until the eleventh century did it become customary for a priest to preside at the latter ceremonies. In the Latin Missal Psalm 128 was utilized for Introit, Gradual, and Communion, with the Alleluia verses from Psalms 20:2 and 134:3, and the Offertory from Psalm 31:14-15a. The new revised Nuptial Mass gives, as choices for the Gradual, Psalm 128 or selected verses from Psalms 33, 34, 103, 112, 145 and 148.

The Lutheran service in *Contemporary Worship* No. 3 lists as suggested Psalms: 33, 100, 117, 127, 128, 136 and 150, to be "sung either by soloist, choir, congregation, or a combination of these" (p. 10). The English Book of Common Prayer has included since 1549 Psalms 128 and 67 in the marriage service; but these were omitted in the American Prayer Book. The proposed, revised service contained in *Services for Trial Use* (1971) suggests between the readings Psalms 128, 113, or 100, "or some other Psalm, Hymn, or Anthem.[144]

Unlike the services for Baptism and Marriage, the rites for the faithful departed have from ancient times made extensive use of the Psalter—in the procession to the grave, the Office of the Dead (Vespers,

Nocturns, Lauds; see Section 14 above), and the Requiem Eucharist. One of the earliest descriptions is in *The Apostolic Constitutions* (ca. 380). Vigils in the cemeteries and the churches were to be observed with lessons, psalms, and Eucharist for the martyrs, all the saints, and the other faithful departed on their anniversaries of death. At funerals of the dead, psalms were to be sung as they were led forth to burial, among which are noted verses 7 and 15 of Psalm 116.[145] In the ancient Latin Requiem, Psalm 65:1-2 was appointed for the Introit, and Psalm 112:6-7 for the Gradual; and in all the chants the common antiphon was one based on 2 Esdras 2:34-35:

Grant them eternal rest, O LORD,
    and let light perpetual shine upon them.

Luther did not prepare a burial service. He had a strong distaste for the medieval Offices and Masses for the dead, with their overtones of "good works" for those in Purgatory. In a booklet published in 1542, "Christian Songs Latin and German, for Use at Funerals," he favored "comforting hymns, of the forgiveness of sins, of rest, of sleep, of life, and of the resurrection of Christians who have died, in order that our faith may be strengthened and the people may be moved to proper devotion." Among these hymns was Luther's metrical version of Psalm 130, "Aus tiefer Not," first published in 1524.[146]

The English Book of Common Prayer of 1549 provided three services for burial: at the grave, an office in the church, and a Requiem Eucharist. At the

Office Psalms 116, 139, and 146 were appointed, and at the Eucharist Psalm 42 as an Introit. All of these Psalms were omitted in the Second Prayer Book of 1552. But the revision of 1661 restored two Psalms to the Office, 39 and 90. These remain in the American Prayer Book, though somewhat shortened, and in addition Psalms 27, 46, 121, and 130; and a special Office for the Burial of a Child includes Psalms 23 and 121. The *Services for Trial Use* (1971) retain Psalms 23 (in two versions), 121, and 130, and suggest in addition Psalms 65:1-8, 116, and 139:1-12.

There is evident much freedom of selection in these traditions, but certain Psalms remain constant: Baptism, 23 and 42; Marriage, 128; and Burial, the *De profundis,* 130.

Notes

1. Cf. Psalm 33:2, 57:8, 92:3, 144:9, and Daniel 3:5 ff.
2. Genesis 49. A similar but later poem on the twelve tribes is the Blessing of Moses in Deuteronomy 33.
3. Exodus 15:21, a song taken up and developed at a later time in the Song of Moses, Exodus 15:1-18.
4. Judges 5:3-31.
5. 2 Samuel 1:19-27 and 3:33-34. Many scholars consider "the last words of David," 2 Samuel 23:1-7, also to be authentic.
6. A collection of these texts, with other documents, may be found in James B. Pritchard, ed., *The Ancient Near East, An Anthology of Texts and Pictures* (Princeton University Press, 1958). This is an abridged edition of the same author's larger two-volume work, *Ancient Near Eastern Texts* and *The Ancient Near East in Pictures* (Princeton University Press, 1954-1955).
7. A translation that attempts to reproduce the alphabetic scheme in English is *The Psalms for Reading and Recitation* (London: Darton, Longman and Todd, 1969), a version which is closely related to the translation of the Psalms in the Jerusalem Bible.
8. The conclusion of the Book of Proverbs (31:10-31) is an acrostic poem in praise of "the good wife."
9. The first four chapters of Lamentations are the oldest and the best acrostic poetry in the Old Testament.
10. An excellent English translation of the Psalter which adheres to a strictly strophic structure of varied patterns, and one that is too little known, is that of Herbert H. Gowen, *The Psalms or The Book of Praises* (Biblical

and Oriental Series; Milwaukee: Morehouse Publishing Co., 1929). To achieve this result, the author employs a radical, but by no means unreasonable, textual criticism.

11. In Psalm 136, the refrain or "praise-shout": "for his mercy endureth for ever," is repeated as the second stich of each verse. A similar use of this refrain is employed in the opening verse or verses of Psalms 106, 107, and 118.

12. One of the best, and still very useful, commentaries of this kind is that edited by A. F. Kirkpatrick, *The Book of Psalms* (The Cambridge Bible for Schools and Colleges; Cambridge University Press, 1902).

13. For an authoritative treatment of this subject, see H. Wheeler Robinson, *Corporate Personality in Ancient Israel* (Facet Books, Biblical Series 11; Philadelphia: Fortress Press, 1964).

14. Most of Gunkel's work on the Psalms is not available in English. A good summary is from one of his encyclopedia articles: *The Psalms, A Form-Critical Introduction*, with an Introduction by James Muilenburg; translated by Thomas M. Horner (Facet Books, Biblical Series 19; Philadelphia: Fortress Press, 1967).

15. Within the Psalter there is a collection, Psalms 120-134, that is entitled "Psalms of Ascents." This group was formed for pilgrims to Jerusalem at the time of the festivals. But it contains Psalms of varied types of praise, lament, and instruction.

16. The only major work of Mowinckel on the Psalms in English is: *The Psalms in Israel's Worship*, Translated by D. R. Ap-Thomas, 2 vols., Oxford: Basil Blackwell, 1962. The principal non-cultic Psalms are: 1, 127 (personal); 106 (penitential meditation); and 19:7-14, 34, 37, 49, 78, 105, 111, 112 (instruction).

17. Gunkel accepted the existence of the festival, but applied to it only Psalms 47, 93, 96-99; Mowinckel applied at least forty.

18. A recent popular introduction to the festival is Donald Anders-Richards, *The Drama of the Psalms*, London: Darton, Longman and Todd, 1968. For an incisive objection, see Roland de Vaux, O. P., *Ancient Israel, Its Life and Institutions*, Translated by John McHugh, New York: McGraw-Hill Book Co., Inc., 1961, pp. 502-506.

19. Ezra 5-6, and the prophets Haggai and Zechariah.
20. Herod's Temple was begun about 20 B.C., and was still in construction in the time of our Lord (cf. John 2:20). For the three Temples, see W. F. Stinespring, "Temple, Jerusalem," *The Interpreter's Dictionary of the Bible,* Vol. IV (1962), pp. 534-560.
21. 1 Chronicles 5:13, 7:3.
22. 1 Chronicles 6:31-48, 15:16-24, 16:4-36, 25:1-7; 2 Chronicles 5:11-13.
23. Psalms 90 to Moses and 72 and 127 to Solomon. In the Greek Version (the Septuagint), Psalms 111, 112, and 138, are assigned to the prophets Haggai and Zechariah.
24. Psalms 3, 7, 18, 34, 51, 52, 54, 56, 57, 59, 60, 63, 142.
25. Psalms 1-2, 10 (which is a continuation of 9), 33, 43, 71, 91, 93-97, 99, 104-107, 111-119, 135-137, 146-150. It will be seen that only six of these occur in the first two Books of the Psalter; the others are in the fourth and fifth Books (see the paragraph following).
26. Psalms 30 for the dedication festival, 92 for the Sabbath, and 100 for the thank-offering. Psalm 45 is a "Love-Song," celebrating a royal wedding. Laments, such as 38 and 70 are simply assigned "For a Memorial" and 102 "For the Afflicted."
27. A good listing and explanation of these notations is that of W. S. McCullough in *The Interpreter's Bible,* Volume IV (1955), pp. 8-10.
28. See the article, with bibliography, by E. Werner, "Musical Instruments," *The Interpreter's Dictionary of the Bible,* Vol. III (1962), pp. 469-476.
29. See the article of I. Sonne, "Synagogue," *The Interpreter's Dictionary of the Bible,* Vol. IV (1962), pp. 476-491.
30. Psalm 74:8 is often cited. This Psalm is a lament over the destruction of the first Temple in 587 B.C.; but verse 8 refers to other shrines, as verse 4 does to the Temple itself. In the Greek Version (Septuagint) the word for "holy place" or "meeting place" in these verses is translated by a word for "festival."
31. Acts 15:21; Philo, *Life of Moses,* iii. 27; Josephus, *Against Apion,* ii. 17.
32. The *Shema,* cited by Jesus in Mark 12:29-30, consists in its fullest form in Deuteronomy 6:4-9, 11:13-21, and Numbers 15:37-41. There is no connection between the

use of this "confession" and that of Creeds in later Christian worship.

33. Numbers 6:24-26.

34. The most detailed and learned study of inter-relationships is that of Eric Werner, *The Sacred Bridge*, New York: Columbia University Press, 1959.

35. Those unable to cope with Eric Werner's book cited in the previous note may find a good synoptic account, with copious bibliography, in his article, "Music," *The Interpreter's Dictionary of the Bible*, Vol. III (1962), pp. 457-469.

36. The Prophets included two groups of writings: 1) The Former Prophets: Joshua, Judges, 1 and 2 Samuel, and 1 and 2 Kings; and 2) The Latter Prophets: Isaiah, Jeremiah, Ezekiel, and the Twelve Minor Prophets.

37. The Greek version, followed by the Latin Vulgate, counts 9 and 10 as one Psalm (correctly, since it is a single acrostic), combines 114 and 115 in one Psalm, and divides into two separate Psalms 116 and 147. Recent Roman Catholic Bibles in English (*e.g.*, the Jerusalem Bible and the New American Bible) now follow the Hebrew enumeration rather than that of the Vulgate.

38. Maccabean dating of Psalms is not popular today. But Psalm 2, an "orphan" royal Psalm, prefatory with Psalm 1 to the entire collection, contains Aramaic expressions, glosses in verses 2, 7, 8, textual uncertainties in verse 11, and an editorial addition to verse 12c. Some scholars find an acrostic in the first ten lines: "To Jannaeus A[lexander] and his wife," that would date its final revision in 103 B.C.

39. See J. A. Sanders, *The Dead Sea Psalms Scroll*, Ithaca: Cornell University Press, 1967.

40. The order of the canonical Psalms is 101-103, 109, 105, 146, 148, 121-132, 119, 135-136, 118, 145, 139, 137-138, 93, 141, 133, 144, 142-143, 149-150, 140, 134. A separate fragment has 118, 104, 147. One will note that all of these Psalms are from Books 4 and 5 of the Psalter, and that the "Songs of Ascents" (minus 120) appear as a unit.

41. Translation of the Scrolls in paperback editions include those of T. H. Gaster (1957), A. Dupont-Sommer (1961), and G. Vermes (1962).

42. C. F. Burney, *The Poetry of Our Lord,* An Examination of the Formal Elements of Hebrew Poetry in the Discourses of Jesus Christ, Oxford: Clarendon Press, 1925.

43. In *Contemporary Worship* 5: Services of the Word (1972), pp. 53-56 and 67, and *Contemporary Worship* 7: Holy Baptism (1974), p. 23, canticles are drawn from Revelation 4:8, 11; 5:9, 12-13; 7:12; and 11:15. In the Episcopalian *Authorized Services 1973,* two canticles added to the Daily Offices are from Revelation 4:11; 5:9-10, 13; and from 15:3-4; pp. 142-143, 169-170. Cf. M. H. Shepherd, Jr., "Hymns," *The Interpreter's Dictionary of the Bible,* Vol. II (1962), pp. 667-668.

44. A list of these quotations is given by A. F. Kirkpatrick, *The Book of Psalms* (Cambridge: University Press, 1902), pp. 838-840; for a slightly different list, see Pius Drijvers, *The Psalms, Their Structure and Meaning* (New York: Herder and Herder, 1964), pp. 261-262. An analysis of these texts is noted in C. A. and E. G. Briggs, *A Critical and Exegetical Commentary on The Book of Psalms* (International Critical Commentary; New York: Scribner's, 1906), pp. ci-cii.

45. Mark 12:1-12=Matthew 21:33-46=Luke 20:9-19; cf. also Acts 4:11 and 1 Peter 2:7.

46. Acts 2:25-35.

47. Acts 13:16-41. The use of Psalm 2:7 as a prophecy of the resurrection is used by Paul himself in Romans 1:4. Some early manuscript readings of Luke 3:22 refer the verse to Jesus' baptism.

48. An example of didactic use is Romans 3:10-18, a cento of verses from Psalms 14, 5, 10, and 36, with inclusion of a citation from Isaiah 59:7-8. Cf. the use of Psalm 34:12-16 in 1 Peter 3:10-12.

49. Especially Psalm 110, cited also in the Gospels and Acts. Verse 1, used as prophetic of Christ's ascension and seating at God's right hand, is reflected in the church's Creeds.

50. Revelation 19:4-7.

51. 2 Samuel 7:12-14; cf. Psalm 132:11-12.

52. Mark 11:9-10; cf. Matthew 21:9, 23:39; Luke 13:35, 19:38; John 12:13.

53. Psalms 22:7-8 and 69:20-21. Other Psalms quoted in the

Passion narratives are: 31:6 (Luke 23:46); 34:20 (John 19:36); 41:9 (John 13:18).

54. Psalm 44:22=Romans 8:36.

55. Cf. Romans 15:9-12, which quotes Psalms 18:49 and 117:1, in conjunction with Deuteronomy 32:43 and Isaiah 11:10.

56. Romans 10:18.

57. John 2:16-21 cites Psalm 69:9 of Christ's Body; for the church as the temple, see 1 Corinthians 3:16-17; 2 Corinthians 6:16; Ephesians 2:19-22; 1 Peter 2:4-5.

58. Revelation 21:2, 22; cf. Galatians 4:25-26; Hebrews 12:22.

59. Acts 2:42-47.

60. 1 Corinthians 14:26.

61. Colossians 3:16-17; cf. Ephesians 5:19-20.

62. *Apology* i. 65-67. The outline of the Eucharistic celebration given by Justin is the basis of all recent revisions of the liturgy today in Western Churches, both Catholic and Protestant. Cf. *Contemporary Worship 2: Services, The Holy Communion* (1970).

63. Tertullian, *On the Soul* 9, 4.

64. Lessons and psalms were chanted by readers and cantors in the Jewish synagogue, and the practice was carried over by the church, except where caution required a quieter rendition of them in times of persecution. For detailed treatment of such "cantillation" see Eric Werner, *The Sacred Bridge* (New York: Columbia University Press, 1959), Part One.

65. Werner, op. cit., p. 131, notes that there is no indication that in the ancient synagogues psalms accompanied the lessons.

66. The "Hallel" Psalms were probably sung by our Lord with his disciples at the Last Supper; cf. the "hymn" in Mark 14:26=Matthew 26:30. For the "Hallel" Psalms at the Jewish Passover, see *The Mishnah,* translated by Herbert Danby (Oxford: Clarendon Press, 1933), p. 151. The same Gradual Psalm is still preserved in the *Service Book and Hymnal* (1958) and in *Contemporary Worship 6: The Church Year* (1973).

67. Psalms 42-43, 46, 67, 80, 107, 118, 136.

68. Psalms 104-106, 111-117, 135, 146-150. The obscure rubric *Selah* that occurs in many psalms is generally understood to refer either to an instrumental interlude

or to a praise-shout by the people—possibly to both. Werner, op. cit., p. 268, considers it comparable to an "Amen."

69. Athanasius, *Defense of His Flight* 24, written in A.D. 357. Similarly, in a Church Order written about 380 in Antioch, and known as the *Apostolic Constitutions* (ii. 57) notes: "When two lessons have been severally read, let some other person sing the hymns of David, and let the people join at the conclusions of the verses." The refrain of Psalm 136 is also found in Psalms 106:1, 107:1, 118:1-4; cf. Ezra 3:10-11; Jeremiah 33:11; 1 Maccabees 4:24.

70. Augustine, *Confessions* x. 33.

71. Gregory the Great, *Letters* v. 57. The translation is from F. Homes Dudden, *Gregory the Great, His Place in History and Thought* (New York: Longmans, Green, and Co., 1905), Vol. I, p. 262.

72. Theodoret, *Church History* ii. 19. Werner, op. cit., p. 176, believes that this form of psalmody was borrowed from the Jewish synagogue. We know that Jewish influence on the church remained strong in Antioch into this period.

73. Socrates, *Church History* vi. 8; Sozomen, *Church History* viii. 8.

74. Augustine, *Confessions* ix. 7. Cf. F. Homes Dudden, *The Life and Times of St. Ambrose* (Oxford: Clarendon Press, 1935), Vol. I, pp. 286, 293-294.

75. *Letter* 207 (translation by Roy J. Deferrari in the edition of the Loeb Classical Library, Harvard University Press: William Heinemann Ltd., Vol. III, p. 187).

76. The most authoritative account of the origins and development of the psalm-chants in the Roman liturgy is by Joseph A. Jungmann, S. J., *The Mass of the Roman Rite* (New York: Benziger Brothers, Inc., 1951, 1955), Vol. I, pp. 320 ff. and 421 ff.; Vol. II, pp. 26 ff. and 391 ff.

77. St. Augustine in his *Retractations,* written in 427, refers to his introduction of Offertory and Communion psalms in North Africa (ii. 37).

78. The oldest monastery in Rome was founded by Pope Sixtus III (432-440), the successor of Pope Celestine, at the Basilica of the Apostles (now St. Sebastian) on the Appian Way, to provide for the Daily Office and

choir at the Eucharist. His successor, Pope Leo I, founded a similar monastery at St. Peter's.

79. Pope Gregory the Great, as already noted, turned over the singing of the Gradual psalm to the *schola*. There is a tradition that he also gave instruction in the school.

80. E.g., the use of Psalm 25 as the Introit on the First Sunday in Advent, and the Second Sunday in Lent. The differing antiphons are still preserved in the *Service Book and Hymnal* (1958) pp. 75 and 84.

81. Theodoret, *Church History* ii. 19; see Jungmann, op. cit., Vol. I, p. 328.

82. For a detailed account of these developments, see Jungmann, op. cit., cited on p. 34, n. 5 above.

83. See Willi Apel, *Harvard Dictionary of Music*, Cambridge: Harvard University Press, 1944, articles: "Neumes," "Notation," and "Plainsong notation."

84. A well-known example of a "trope" in the Anglican Prayer Book is that of the *Kyrie eleison*, as it is adapted in response to the recital of the Ten Commandments: "Lord, have mercy upon us, and incline our hearts to keep this law." Cf. Luther's metrical version of the Commandments (1524): "Dies sind die heiligen zehn Gebot," with its refrain *Kyrieleis*.

85. Many translations of medieval Sequence hymns have found their way into modern hymnals. Two late medieval vernacular adaptations of the Easter and Pentecost Sequences have continued to be popular in Lutheran churches: "Christ ist erstanden" (Easter) and "Komm heiliger Geist, Herre Gott" (Pentecost); cf. *The Service Book and Hymnal* (1958), Nos. 107 and 122.

86. Luther D. Reed, *The Lutheran Liturgy,* Revised edition, Philadelphia: Muhlenberg [now Fortress] Press, 1959, p. 78.

87. The best account in English of the development of the French Psalter of 1562, with a transcription of all the melodies in modern notation, is that of Waldo Selden Pratt, *The Music of the French Psalter of 1562,* New York: Columbia University Press, 1939.

88. The most widely known and used of Bourgeois' melodies is "Old Hundredth"—actually the tune which is provided for the metrical French version of Psalm 134. In the *Service Book and Hymnal* (1958) another Bour-

geois tune is included (No. 220), the one he composed
for Marot's metrical version of the *Nunc Dimittis.*
89. The history of English metrical psalmody and hymnody
has been frequently recounted. Good introductions may
be found in such standard works as John Julian's *A
Dictionary of Hymnology,* and the article "Psalter" in
the various editions of *Grove's Dictionary of Music and
Musicians.*
90. Henry Gee and William John Hardy, *Documents Illustrative of English Church History,* London: Macmillan
and Co., Ltd., 1896, p. 435.
91. Psalm 54:17; Daniel 6:10; Acts 2:15, 3:1, 10:3, 9, 30.
92. By the third century, certain churches had weekday
services, which, if not the Eucharist, were a *synaxis*
("gathering") for hearing the Scriptures read and interpreted.
93. Mark 13:33-37; cf. Matthew 24:42, 25:13; Luke
12:38-40.
94. *The Treatise on The Apostolic Tradition of St Hippolytus of Rome,* Edited by Gregory Dix, London: S.P.C.K.,
1937, pp. 61-67. The scheme is basically that of Mark's
Gospel, with some reminiscences of Matthew and John.
Only Mark states specifically that Jesus was crucified
at the third hour (15:25).
95. Other third century Fathers, such as Tertullian and
Cyprian, have a similar scheme; but they associate the
third hour also with the gift of the Holy Spirit at Pentecost (Acts 2:15) or the sixth hour with the crucifixion
(cf. John 19:14). Other reminiscences were the conversion of St. Paul and the vision of St. Peter at noon
(Acts 22:6, 10:9).
96. Cassian is our principal source for these early arrangements of the Offices, in his *Institutes,* books ii and iii.
See Owen Chadwick, *John Cassian, A Study in Primitive
Monasticism,* Cambridge: University Press, 1950, pp.
63-70.
97. W. K. L. Clarke, *The Ascetic Works of Saint Basil*
(Translations of Christian Literature, Series I. Greek
Texts), London: S.P.C.K., 1925, pp. 207-209.
98. Cf. Pierre Salmon, *The Breviary Through the Centuries,*
Collegeville, Minn.: The Liturgical Press, 1962, p. 5.
99. ii. 59; cf. viii. 34-39.
100. *Institutes* iii. 6.

101. Chapter 13. The more specific assignment of Psalms at Lauds in the *Rule* may well reflect custom at Rome.
102. M. L. McClure and C. L. Feltoe, *The Pilgrimage of Etheria* (Translations of Christian Literature, Series III: Liturgical Texts), London: S.P.C.K., n.d., pp. 45 ff.
103. Salmon, op. cit., pp. 5 ff., 28 ff.; for more detailed treatment, see S. J. P. Van Dijk, O. F. M., and J. Hazelden Walker, *The Origins of the Modern Roman Liturgy,* Westminster: The Newman Press, 1960, Chapter One.
104. Cf. Ruth 2:4; the response in this verse, "The Lord bless you" has a parallel in Psalm 129:8.
105. Cf. Psalm 118:1; also 106:1, 107:1, 136:1.
106. The translation of this verse in the *Service Book and Hymnal* of 1958 is that of the King James Version.
107. Many of these texts for the several seasons of the Church Year are included in the *Service Book and Hymnal* of 1958, pp. 149-152. In the Anglican Prayer Books they have all been excluded; though recent revisions have restored "invitatories" (i.e., antiphons) for certain seasons and days of the *Venite*, Psalm 95.
108. The first two sections of the *Te Deum* were probably composed in the West in the fourth century. The third section of versicles is later, since the Scriptural text used is the Vulgate, not the Old Latin version cited in the first two sections.
109. Cf. *Service Book and Hymnal* of 1958, pp. 153-156. The Anglican versicles are based upon older vernacular ones of late medieval times used in the procession on Sundays.
110. For the history of these devotions, see Edmund Bishop, "On the Origin of the Prymer," *Liturgica Historica,* Oxford University Press, 1918, pp. 211-237; and J. B. L. Tolhurst, *The Monastic Breviary of Hyde Abbey, Winchester,* London: Henry Bradshaw Society, 1942.
111. Quignonez' Breviary was very influential upon Archbishop Thomas Cranmer in his revision of the Daily Offices for the Church of England. The preface of the First Book of Common Prayer of 1549 quotes many passages from Quignonez' preface.
112. The constant increase of saints' days with privileged propers in the course of time resulted in the same disruption of the regular course of psalmody, as in the Middle Ages. Hence a new distribution for the week

was made by Pope Pius X in 1911. See John H. Miller, C.S.C., *Fundamentals of the Liturgy*, Notre Dame; Fides Publishers Association, 1959, pp. 319-329.

113. *The Lutheran Liturgy*, Revised Edition, Philadelphia: Muhlenberg (Fortress) Press, 1959, p. 394.

114. Later revisions of the Prayer Book in both the English and other Anglican churches have greatly modified the wooden course reading of the Psalms once a month. Proper Psalms have been appointed for Sundays and major Holy Days; and in recent revisions the course of Psalm reading on weekdays has been spread over a period of about six weeks, with some Psalms appointed more frequently than others.

115. An excellent modern Lutheran adaptation is that of Herbert Lindemann, *The Daily Office. . . .* Designed for Private Devotion and Group Worship, St. Louis: Concordia Publishing House, 1965.

116. The Indian Prayer Book also includes "A Liturgy for India," first developed in the Diocese of Bombay in 1920 and revised in 1933. This included a lectionary of three lessons with a proper Psalm: *The Supplement to the Book of Common Prayer*, Madras-Delhi-Lahore: I.S.P.C.K., 1961, pp. 253-267. The 1933 Liturgy of the Church in Ceylon also allowed a "Psalm or Hymn" for Introit, Gradual, Offertory, and Communion.

117. *The Calendar and Lessons for the Church's Year*, London: S.P.C.K., 1969.

118. *Services for Trial Use*, Authorized Alternatives to Prayer Book Services, New York: The Church Hymnal Corporation, 1971, pp. 473 ff.; reprinted with some revision in *Authorized Services* 1973, pp. 649 ff.

119. *The Worshipbook, Services and Hymns*, Philadelphia: The Westminster Press, 1970, pp. 135-163; the book does not include, however, the texts of these "Responsive Readings."

120. The discrepancies are principally in the assignment of Gospels for the Sundays in Advent, and in the shift of one week during the post-Pentecost (Trinity) season of the Gospel lesson from the Epistle with which it was originally associated.

121. Translation in Walter M. Abbott, S. J., ed., *The Documents of Vatican II*, pp. 155, 169. Reprinted with permission of America Press. All rights reserved. © 1966

by America Press, 106 N. 56 Street, New York, NY 10019.

122. The Consilium invited six non-Roman Catholic Observers to attend its sessions and confer with its committees. Of these six, two were Lutherans and two were Anglicans. The Lutheran Observers were the Rev. Dr. F. W. Künneth of the Lutheran World Federation, and the Rev. Dr. Eugene L. Brand of the American Lutheran Church.

123. For introduction to the three year cycle, see *Contemporary Worship 6, The Church Year* (1973), pp. 17-24; *The Church Year* (Prayer Book Studies 19), New York: The Church Hymnal Corporation, 1970, pp. 46-53. The Presbyterian adaptation will be found in *The Worshipbook* of 1970, pp. 166-175.

124. *Contemporary Worship 6, The Church Year* (1973), pp. 28-29.

125. *The Cambridge History of the Bible. The West from the Reformation to the Present Day.* Edited by S. L. Greenslade. Cambridge: University Press, 1963, pp. 94-174, 339-382.

126. Ronald Knox, *The Psalms, A New Translation,* New York: Sheed and Ward, 1947; *The Psalms in Rhythmic Prose,* Translated by James A. Kleist, S. J., and Thomas J. Lynam, S. J., Milwaukee: The Bruce Publishing Co., 1954; *The Psalms* (Fides Translation), Introduction and Notes by Mary Perkins Ryan, Chicago: Fides Publishers, 1955.

127. The Grail text (1963) is published in the United States as *The Psalms, A New Translation,* Philadelphia: The Westminster Press. This does not contain the antiphons of the musical settings.

128. *The Psalms in Modern Speech* 3 vols., Philadelphia: Fortress Press, 1968. Both this translation and The Grail version attempt to preserve in English the tonal rhythms of the original Hebrew.

129. *The Revised Psalter,* London: S.P.C.K., 1964; *The Prayer Book Psalter Revised,* New York: The Church Hymnal Corporation, 1973 (the text also reprinted in *Authorized Services 1973* by the same publisher).

130. The project began with the translation of the New Testament, published in 1966, under the title *Good News for Modern Man.*

131. *Fifty Psalms, An Attempt at a New Translation,* London: Burns and Oates Ltd., 1968. The original Dutch was prepared by Huub Oosterhuis, Michael van der Plas, Pius Drijvers, and Han Renckens; the English edition by Frans Josef van Beeck, David Smith, and Forrest Ingram.

132. A good list of anthem settings, but by no means exhaustive, is that of Paul Foelber, "CW-6 Psalm Settings," *Response in Worship, Music, and the Arts,* Vol. XIII, No. 3 (1973), pp. 15-24.

133. Unison chants, such as plainsong, generally range within a fifth of the scale; harmonized chants, such as Anglican chant, range an octave or more. But anything beyond an octave is uncomfortable for congregations.

134. To achieve good rhythm, one should rehearse the Psalm verses by reading aloud, then transferring the reading rhythm to a monotone, and finally reproducing it in the melody of the chant.

135. The intonation is normally used only in the first verse; but in more elaborated melodies it may be used with each verse.

136. In many churches, where the Psalms are read and not sung, there is a custom of breaking the antiphonal reading at the half-verse. This leads to a choppy effect, and is impossible musically. It is important for rhythm and sense that a whole verse be said at one time, pausing for a silent beat after the half-verse.

137. This may take the form of descant to the melody, or what is called *faux-bourdon*. In the latter, the melody of the chant is in the tenor, and the other voices weave about it a harmonic or polyphonic texture. The "Festal Preces" of Evening Prayer in *The Hymnal 1940* (Episcopalian), No. 602, are treated in this way. In the *Service Book and Hymnal* of 1958 there is an example in the setting of the *Gloria Patri* on p. 129.

138. The most complete and learned introduction is that of Willi Apel, *Gregorian Chant,* Bloomington, Indiana University Press, 1958.

139. A few fragments have survived of ancient Gallican chant, and some manuscripts of Mozarabic (Spanish) chant, but these are largely not decipherable. The Ambrosian chant is still a living tradition in the church of Milan, but it is not easily accessible.

140. *En Route,* Translated by C. Kegan Paul, New York: E. P. Dutton and Co., 1920, p. 246; quoted with approval by Cecil Gray, *The History of Music,* 2nd ed. rev., New York: Alfred A. Knopf, 1935, p. 24.

141. *Crisis in Church Music?* Proceedings of a meeting on church music conducted by The Liturgical Conference and The Church Music Association of America, Washington: The Liturgical Conference, 1967, pp. 11-12. Quoted by permission of The Liturgical Conference. All of the twelve essays in this volume are provocative in the varying views about traditional and modern liturgical music.

142. The harmonized chants for Psalms and canticles in both the Episcopal *Hymnal 1940* and the Lutheran *Service Book and Hymnal* of 1958 exhibit in their pointing a mixture of the two methods.

143. The Book of Common Prayer directs that Baptism be administered, except for urgent cause, after the second lesson of Morning or Evening Prayer; but no proper Psalms are appointed for such occasions.

144. At the present time when couples are concerned to limit the size of their families, such Psalms as 127 and 128 may not be very acceptable.

145. vi. 30, viii. 41-42.

146. See *Service Book and Hymnal* of 1958, No. 372.

Bibliography

A. The Study of the Psalter

Translations

In addition to the recent Bible translations in current use: The Revised Standard Version, The Jerusalem Bible, The New English Bible, and The New American Bible—the following translations of the Psalter may be consulted:

The Psalms, A New Translation. Translated from the Hebrew and arranged for Singing to the Psalmody of Joseph Gelineau. (The Grail.) Philadelphia: The Westminster Press, 1963.

The Psalms in Modern Speech. For Public and Private Use. By Richard S. Hanson. 3 vols. Philadelphia: Fortress Press, 1968.

The Psalms for Modern Man. New York: American Bible Society, 1970. [Designed for those of a limited English vocabulary.]

The Prayer Book Psalter Revised. New York: The Church Hymnal Corporation, 1973. [Prepared for the Standing Liturgical Commission of the Episcopal Church; reproduced in *Authorized Services 1973*, New York: The Church Hymnal Corporation, 1973.]

Introductions

Basic introductions may be consulted in all the major commentaries (see below) or in the standard dictionaries of the Bible, such as *The Interpreter's Dictionary of the Bible,* 4 vols., New York-Nashville: Abingdon Press, 1962; James Hastings, *Dictionary of the Bible,* Revised edition, New York: Charles Scribner's Sons, 1963.

Barth, Christoph F., *Introduction to the Psalms.* Translated by R. A. Wilson. New York: Scribner's, 1966.

Drijvers, Pius, O. C. S. O., *The Psalms, Their Structure and Meaning.* London: Burns and Oates, 1965. [Excellent; based on Gunkel's work, but concerned with religion of the Psalms and relevance to Christian understanding.]

Gunkel, Hermann, *The Psalms, A Form-Critical Introduction.* With an Introduction by James Muilenburg. Translated by Thomas M. Horner. (Facet Books—Biblical Series 19.) Philadelphia: Fortress Press, 1967. [Fundamental; with an excellent bibliography.]

Guthrie, Harvey H., Jr., *Israel's Sacred Songs, A Study of Dominant Themes.* New York: The Seabury Press, 1966.

Paterson, John, *The Praises of Israel.* Studies Literary and Religious in the Psalms. New York: Scribner's, 1950. [One of the best in English.]

Terrien, Samuel, *The Psalms and Their Meaning for Today.* Indianapolis and New York: The Bobbs-Merrill Co., Inc., 1952.

Westermann, Claus, *The Praise of God in the Psalms.* Translated by Keith R. Crim. Richmond: John Knox Press, 1965.

Commentaries

Briggs, Charles Augustus, and Emilie Grace, *A Critical and Exegetical Commentary on the Book of Psalms.* 2 vols. (The International Critical Commentary.) Edinburgh: T. and T. Clark, 1906-1907. [The most exhaustive and learned commentary in English; radical in textual criticism.]

Kirkpatrick, A. F., *The Book of Psalms*. (The Cambridge Bible for Schools and Colleges.) Cambridge: University Press, 1902. [Based on King James Version, but critical though conservative; excellent cross-references to related Bible passages.]

Leslie, Elmer A., *The Psalms Translated and Interpreted in the Light of Hebrew Life and Worship*. New York: Abingdon Press, 1949.

McCullough, W. Stewart, and Taylor, William R., "The Book of Psalms," *The Interpreter's Bible*, Vol. IV. New York: Abingdon Press, 1955, pp. 3-763. [Uneven in quality.]

Oesterley, W. O. E., *The Psalms*. Translated with Text-Critical and Exegetical Notes. 2 vols. London: S.P.C.K., 1939.

Toombs, Lawrence E., "The Psalms," *The Interpreter's One-Volume Commentary on the Bible*. Edited by Charles M. Laymon. Nashville—New York: Abingdon Press, 1971, pp. 253-303. [Introduction and notes for general student.]

Weiser, Anton, *The Psalms, A Commentary*. (The Old Testament Library.) Philadelphia: The Westminster Press, 1962. [Much favored today as an all-round commentary.]

Special Studies

Gray, George Buchanan, *The Forms of Hebrew Poetry, Considered with Special Reference to the Criticism and Interpretation of the Old Testament*. London: Hodder and Stoughton, 1915. [The standard work on Hebrew Poetry.]

Johnson, Aubrey R., *Sacral Kingship in Ancient Israel*. Cardiff: University of Wales Press, 1955. [On the cultus implicit in the "royal" Psalms.]

Mowinckel, Sigmund, *The Psalms in Israel's Worship*. Translated by D. R. Ap-Thomas. 2 vols. Oxford: Basil Blackwell, 1962. [A work of great influence with respect to the cultic background of the Psalms.]

Robinson, Theodore W., *The Poetry of the Old Testament*. (Studies in Theology.) New York: Scribner's, 1947.

Werner, Eric, *The Sacred Bridge, The Interdependence of Liturgy and Music in Synagogue and Church during the First Millenium*. New York: Columbia University Press, 1959. [The most exhaustive and learned study of the subject.]

Christian Use of the Psalms

de Candole, Henry, *The Christian Use of the Psalms*. London: A. R. Mowbray and Co., Ltd., 1955. [A brief introduction.]

Douglas, Winfred, *Church Music in History and Practice*. Revised with Additional Material by Leonard Ellinwood. New York: Scribner's, 1962. [Designed for history and background of Anglican liturgy.]

Jungmann, Joseph A., S. J., *The Mass of the Roman Rite, Its Origins and Development*. Translated by Francis A. Brunner, C.SS.R. 2 vols. New York: Benziger Brothers, Inc., 1951, 1955. [The most authoritative work on the subject.]

Lamb, John Alexander, *The Psalms in Christian Worship*. London: The Faith Press, 1962. [A historical survey.]

Reed, Luther D., *The Lutheran Liturgy*. Revised edition. Philadelphia: Muhlenberg [Fortress] Press, 1959. [See Index: "Psalm."]

Scott, R. B. Y., *The Psalms as Christian Psalms*. (World Christian Books No. 24.) London: Lutterworth Press, 1958.

Worden, T., *The Psalms Are Christian Prayer*. New York: Sheed and Ward, 1961. [A Sensitive, insightful and critical interpretation.]

B. Musical Settings Old and New

Plainsong

Complete Psalters (without antiphons)

> *The Plainsong Psalter.* The Psalms of David according to the American Book of Common Prayer, Pointed and Set to Gregorian Chants by The Joint Commission on Church Music, under the authority of General Convention. New York: The H. W. Gray Co., 1932. [Text from the 1928 American Prayer Book.]

> Groom, Lester, *Accompanying Harmonies for the Plainsong Psalter.* New York: The H. W. Gray Co., Inc., 1933. [A companion to the preceding, which provided only melodies.]

> Lindemann, Herbert, *The Psalter of the Authorized Version of the Scriptures.* Minneapolis: Augsburg Publishing House, 1940.

Psalms for Seasonal and Sunday Propers (with antiphons)

> *The Sunday Psalter.* Psalms for Sundays and Feast Days Set to the Psalm Tones and Provided with Proper Antiphons. Compiled and Adapted by Herbert Lindemann. Edited and Harmonized by Newman W. Powell. St. Louis: Concordia Publishing House, 1961. [A Standard, competent work.]

> Bunjes, Paul, *The Service Propers Noted.* The Introits and Intervenient Chants for the Sundays, Feasts and Occasions of the Liturgical Year Set to Formulary

Tones. Authorized by the Commission on Worship, Liturgics, and Hymnology of The Lutheran Church —Missouri Synod. St. Louis: Concordia Publishing House, 1960. [Original melodies composed in the manner and modes of plainsong. Designed for choirs. The same publishing house also issued the author's two volumes of Accompaniments (1960) and *The Formulary Tones Annotated* (1965).]

Christensen, Albert Olai, and Schuneman, Harold Edward, *Proper of the Services. For the Church Year.* Set to Gregorian Psalm-Tones with Organ Accompaniment. New York: The H. W. Gray Co., Inc., 1947. [Propers of the Common Service Book of the United Lutheran Church and The Lutheran Hymnal of the Evangelical Lutheran Synodical Conference. Includes also Offertories. For congregational or choir use.]

Ensrud, Paul, *Introits and Graduals for the Lutheran Service.* Series A, Psalm Tone Settings. 6 vols. Minneapolis: Augsburg Publishing House, 1960-1964. [Simple Psalm tone settings, almost syllabic, with antiphons in the same tones, but with an intonation. Easy for congregations.]

Frischmann, Charles, *The Psalmody of the Day.* Series A with Seasonal Psalms for Entrance and Communion. Philadelphia: Fortress Press, 1974. [For Year A in the new lectionary of the Inter-Lutheran Commission on Worship. Four Psalm tones are used, with antiphons or refrains in two-part or four-part harmony of a more metrical character and appointed after each verse. The refrains are designed for congregations. Settings for Year B and for the Lesser Festivals were published in 1975.]

Vogel, Dwight W., *The Psalms for Worship Today.* St. Louis: Concordia Publishing House, 1974. [Arranged by subject matter, with tables suggesting use in the Church Year. For various combinations of cantor, choir, and congregation. The text is the American Bible Society's *The Psalms for Modern Man* (1970).]

Willan, Healey, *Graduals for the Church Year*. St. Louis: Concordia Publishing House, 1960. [Only the Tracts for Pre-Lent and Lent are set to Psalm tones; otherwise the Graduals and Alleluias are in four-part harmony for choirs, with optional, light accompaniment. The texts are from the *Common Service*.]

Harmonized Chants

The American Psalter. The Psalms and Canticles . . . Pointed and Set to Anglican Chants together with The Choral Service. Prepared by The Joint Commission on Church Music. New York: The H. W. Gray Co., 1930. [The pointing is based upon plainsong, so that the final note of the cadence has only one syllable. Text from the American Book of Common Prayer 1928.]

The Choral Psalter. Edited by G. T. Thalben-Ball. London: Ernest Benn, Ltd., 1957. [Text from the English Prayer Book. Chants treated with greater flexibility to suit the text.]

The Oxford Psalter. Containing The Psalms, together with The Canticles and Hymns, The Litany (1544) and Proper Psalms for Certain Days. Newly Pointed for Chanting and Edited by Henry G. Ley, E. Stanley Roper, and C. Hylton Stewart. Oxford University Press, 1929. 2nd edition, 1936. [Text from the English Prayer Book. There is no music, but texts are pointed by the "speech rhythm" developed at the Royal College of Church Music.]

The Oxford American Psalter. Pointed and Set to Anglican Chants by Ray F. Brown. New York: Oxford University Press, 1949. [Pointing based on that of *The Oxford Psalter* above.]

The Scottish Psalter. London: Oxford University Press, 1929. [The Authorized Version pointed to Anglican chants.]

Anthems of the Day. Scriptural Verses Set to Anglican

Chant and Plainsong. By Morton C. Stone and Ray
F. Brown. New York: Oxford University Press, 1952.
[Four Scriptural texts, including many from the
Psalms, for use as propers on Sundays and major
holy days. The texts are unofficial, but are permitted
under the rubrics of the American Book of Common
Prayer 1928.]

Gilbert, Harold W., *Introits and Graduals for the
Church Year*. Set to music and pointed for Speech
Rhythm Singing. 2 vols. Philadelphia: Fortress
Press, 1964. [Texts from the *Service Book and Hymnal* of 1958. For choir use, with conventional Anglican chants for the *Gloria Patri*. A Supplement provides Organ Modulations from Introit to Kyrie.]

Harmonized Metrical Psalmody

Most Hymnals contain harmonized metrical translations or paraphrases based on the Psalms. The *Service Book and Hymnal* (1958), page 284, lists those
contained in this Hymnal.

Connaughton, Luke, and Mayhew, Kevin, *Songs from
the Psalms*. London: The Young Christian Workers,
1966. [American outlet: The Liturgical Press, Collegeville. Twelve metrical Psalms set to simple
melodies for congregational use, with accompaniment.]

Schütz, Heinrich, *Ten Psalms from the "Becker Psalter"
1628*. Edited and Translated by Robert E. Wunder-
lich. St. Louis: Concordia Publishing House, 1958.
[Both chorale and polyphonic forms. *Ten More
Psalms* have been published in 1968.]

"Gelineau" Psalmody

The Grail/Gelineau Psalter. Chicago: G. I. A. Publications, Inc., 1974 [Contains all 150 Psalms to "Gelineau" melodies, but without antiphons. With accompaniments.] Earlier editions in melody or with accompaniment and choir parts:

Twenty Four Psalms and a Canticle. [Magnificat]
Thirty Psalms and Two Canticles. [Nunc Dimittis and Benedictus]
Twenty Psalms and Three Canticles. [Blessings from the Book of Daniel, Canticle of Zachary, Canticle of the Three Children]

Psalmody based on Gelineau

Arthur, John, *Prayers, Psalms and Days' Songs.* Chicago: Lutheran Council in the USA, 1970. [Original translations based on the Jerusalem Bible and Hanson. Fifteen original tunes in three different meters and four line stanzas. Selected and arranged according to the Church Year—some traditional, some by the author—for use before the last lection, for unison, congregational singing. Includes Alleluia verses. Tonalities in major and minor modes. More rigidly metrical and less varied than those of Gelineau.]

Hughes, Howard, S. M., *Psalms for Advent.* An Entrance Psalm, the Psalm Responses from the Lectionary (A, B, and C) and the Gospel Acclamation Verses for each Sunday in Advent. Chicago: G. I. A. Publications, Inc., 1970. [Texts from the New American Bible. Antiphons in 2/2 or 4/4 meter for the congregation, with more free melodies for the Psalm verses for a cantor. Accompaniments light and not difficult; melodies in range of a fifth; more recitative than in Gelineau. Excellent for small choirs and congregations.]

Roff, Joseph, *Seasonal Responsorial Psalms.* For Cantor and Congregation with Optional SATB Choir and Organ. Chicago: G. I. A. Publications, Inc., 1972. [Texts from New American Bible, one set per season. Metrical, with antiphons in unison or harmony for congregation and choir. Psalm verses in unison for cantor or choir. Range moderate, accompaniment light; antiphons of varied melodic interest, but Psalm verses more like recitative. Good for small choirs and congregations.

Somerville, S., *Psalms for Singing*. Book One. Cincinnati: World Library of Sacred Music, 1960. [Contains fourteen Psalms, with simpler and less interesting melodies than those of Gelineau. Non-metrical; reciting notes have various numbers of syllables. Translations from the Latin Psalter of 1945. Organ accompaniment available.]

The Simple Gradual for Sundays and Holy Days. Full Music Edition for Cantor, Choir and Organist. Edited by John Ainslie. London: Geoffrey Chapman Ltd., 1970. [Approved English texts of the *Graduale Simplex*, with the antiphons and refrains, with full directions as to rendition. Responsorial Psalms and Alleluias to chants by Dom Laurence Bévenot and the Editor; Entrance, Offertory and Communion Songs to chants by Joseph Gelineau, Dom Bénevot, and Dom Gregory Murray.]

Mixed Types

Songs for Liturgy and More Hymns and Spiritual Songs. Prepared by the Joint Commission on Church Music of the Episcopal Church. Walton Music Corporation, 1971. [Designed for trial use services of the Episcopal Church, with both unison and accompaniment editions. Includes ten selections from the Psalms, some in plainsong, some in modern compositions—the latter ones more difficult and hence more suitable for choirs.]

Deiss, Lucien, C.C.Sp., *Biblical Hymns and Psalms*. 2 vols. Cincinnati: World Library Publications, Inc., 1965, 1971. [Originally in French; translations by the author. Many Psalms are scattered through these volumes, in various styles, but uneven in quality. Antiphons for the congregation, some of them in harmony, with Psalm verses for cantors or choir. Popular in Roman Catholic churches.]

Jerome, Peter, *Psalms for Singing*. Seven Tunes for Twelve Psalms. Dallas: Choristers Guild, 1972. [Only a few verses of each Psalm are provided in

strong rhythmical melodies. Accompaniment provided for piano, with suggestions for handbells,
clapping or percussion instruments. Choir; or with
frequent use easily learned by congregations.]

Martens, Mason, *Music for the Holy Eucharist and the
Daily Office*. New York: The Church Army in the
U.S.A., 1971. [Traditional and new melodies designed for trial use services in the Episcopal Church.
Includes settings of 25 selections from the Psalms,
some in plainsong, some in metrical measures. Antiphons sung by congregation, Psalm verses by cantor. Simple and easily learned. No accompaniment.]

Peloquin, C. A., *Songs of Israel*. Seasonal Responsorial
Psalms for the Entire Year. For Cantor and Congregation with Optional Choir, Accompanied. Chicago:
G. I. A. Publications, Inc., 1971. [By one of the most
original of contemporary Roman Catholic composers.
Except for the relatively simple antiphons for the
congregation, these seasonal selections would be
considered anthems. Accompaniments are difficult,
and the Psalm verses for cantors require excellent
singers. Great variety and vitality.]

Storey, Williams G., Quinn, Frank C., O. P., and
Wright, David F., O. P., *Morning Praise and Even-
song*. A Liturgy of the Hours in Musical Setting.
Notre Dame: Fides Publishers, Inc., 1973. [Adapta-
tions of the Roman Catholic Daily Offices for congregational use. Psalms and canticles scattered
through the book are admirably suited to this purpose. Many Psalms are in metrical versions from
the old metrical Psalters; others are in forms similar
to the Gelineau psalmody.]

Wetzler, Robert, *Introits*. 5 parts. Minneapolis: Augsburg Publishing House, 1964-1965. [Original compositions for the Introit propers in the *Service Book
and Hymnal* (1958). Essentially designed for choirs,
often with women's and men's voices employed
contrapuntally. Accompaniments on the more difficult side. Originality and rhythmic interest.]